'A new era has come for the ch[...]
kingdom of God. In this ep[...]
beyond the walls of chur[...]
communities, homes and relev[...]
true salt and light, we are the spice and seasoning for the
world to "taste and see that God is good"! This is the spirit
of this fantastic book written by Liz with such humility,
vulnerability and clarity. May its contents change the way
many believers engage more widely with the world, in the
true love and spirit of Jesus.'
Dr Jonathan Oloyede, National Day of Prayer UK

'This book is a powerful challenge to put Christian unity
into action. It embraces all that is great about churches
praying and working together, but it goes much further –
it pushes Christians beyond their church-shaped boxes and
out into their communities, where they truly belong and
where they can bring hope. In this book, Elizabeth and
Mick not only show their passion for unity, they also show
that unity should always have purpose, reaching out and
bringing change. Packed with practical suggestions, I
highly recommend this book for all unity movements who
want to see real, sustainable change in their places.'
*Ian Mayer, author and entrepreneur working with community
leaders for social transformation*

'This book very helpfully underlines the key tenets of the
growing city transformation movement around the world.
This is a passionate call to the unity of the Body of Christ,
underlined by sustained prayer that results in effective
strategic incarnational mission. This story of God's activity

in Barking is being replicated in Dallas, Mumbai, Berlin, Sunderland, Pretoria and many other cities around the world. God is working for social, cultural and spiritual kingdom transformation of all cities and places. Get this book and catch the vision and be part of this extraordinary move of God.'

Rev Roger Sutton, author of Gathering Momentum and Director of Gather www.gather.global and Movement Day UK www.movementday.uk

Jesus
in Town

Elizabeth Mednick

instant
ap[ ]stle

First published in Great Britain in 2019.

Instant Apostle
The Barn
1 Watford House Lane
Watford
Herts
WD17 1BJ

if notified, will formally seek permission at the earliest opportunity.

The views and opinions expressed in this work are those of the author and do not necessarily reflect the views and opinions of the publisher.

British Library Cataloguing-in-Publication Data

A catalogue record for this book is available from the British Library

This book and all other Instant Apostle books are available from Instant Apostle:

Website: www.instantapostle.com

E-mail: info@instantapostle.com

ISBN 978-1-912726-02-8

Printed in Great Britain.

Dedication

To the glory of God in Barking and to those Christians who have faithfully responded to His call to serve the unity of the church in Barking.

Contents

Foreword

This is the story of the establishing of an organisation called Barking Churches Unite (BCU) and how it seeks to work in the town of Barking, Essex, to show God's love to the residents by meeting needs, especially among the poor.

I don't know exactly when I had the idea for this book; I only knew that someone had to write down all the wonderful things that have been happening in Barking. I started jotting ideas down as they occurred and writing accounts of specific times of God's working or revelation. Some months there has been a lot of information, at other times there have been long gaps.

In the few years leading up to autumn 2014, a number of significant life events prevented me from working on this book. My husband Mick's father died in 2010. Then Mick was made redundant from the education support service where he had been working for eight years, and was unemployed for four months. Interestingly, this was around the time when his brother developed cancer and Mick was free to take him to hospital every day and to be a support to him in a way that would have been impossible had he been working. (God's timing is always right!)

In 2011 our daughter, Melody, was married, with much of the angst that the organisation of a wedding sometimes produces. The following year my mother broke her leg and spent four months in hospital, where she died in March 2013.

Perhaps because of these events, I had been feeling rather discouraged and not able to write. In addition, our ideas and plans for work in the community were held back by lack of support and lack of funding, and people seemed unable to follow through on promises – a bit like my own writer's block! However, in spite of these and my family situations, I kept coming back to my task of recording events as they occurred in the hope of putting them into a coherent form when I had the time.

Eventually I decided that enough time had elapsed since we started the venture and established Barking Churches Unite. It was time to stop recording events; I could go on for ever. The year we became a charity, 2017, seemed to be an appropriate time to stop and take a good look at what God has done for and through us. So here is the account of our first seven years of unexpected surprises, disappointments, hope, prayers, laughter and marvellous unity, new friendships and close Christian love and fellowship. May God continue to bless the work as we depend on His grace, guidance and provision of resources and money.

Introduction
Joining the dots (God paints a picture)

I am lying in a sleeping bag on a mattress on the floor in semi-darkness in a large, warm church hall, listening to various people snoring. On the floor next to me is a pair of shoes, and my small bag of belongings is on a chair. I have just cooked dinner for twelve people in a well-equipped church kitchen, and I compare it favourably with some of the other kitchens I use. I am only here for one night; in the morning I will return to my comfortable house. I am one of the volunteers at the Barking Churches Unite night shelter.

We have ten guests here tonight, who are currently homeless in Barking and Dagenham. They come from many strata of society and have different ethnic origins. We as churches in the area are providing a night shelter for the winter.

Homelessness, loneliness, poverty, hunger, sickness: these are all around us in society and in our churches. What can the church as a body do to alleviate some of these things and to show the love of God to people outside? When churches work together, amazing things can be achieved.

In Barking and Dagenham we believe we have been shown a 'blueprint' from God as to how we can make a difference to the lives of some of the people we encounter.

This is the story of how God has led us step by step to represent His love to people in the community.

Joining the dots

Why 'Joining the dots'? Only God sees the big picture of our lives and circumstances, and He sees the needs in the world that Christians ought to be meeting. There are two ways of looking at the phrase. The first relates to our own spiritual journey. A beautiful picture can only be made by first having an outline of dots and then it can be filled with colour. Only God knows what the picture will portray. We have to be willing to wield the pencil, one dot at a time, as God reveals each new number of the outline as our personal journey emerges. We trust God for one step at a time. As He reveals the next step, or dot, the picture is revealed.

The second interpretation relates to the larger picture of the world. The 'dots' resemble the people and circumstances that God links together to form His outline and picture. We have encountered this time and time again as God has revealed His plans for the work in Barking.

Our personal background

My husband, Mick, grew up in a non-Christian home in Barking, Essex, and his father was a shopkeeper who owned a launderette and another small business. He fully expected Mick to follow in his footsteps and continue the businesses on leaving school, but God had other ideas. Soon after his parents divorced, when Mick was thirteen, he became a Christian while he was at a Boys' Brigade camp. Mick knew in his teens that he wanted to teach in special needs education and duly enrolled in a teaching course in 1978, encouraged by his mother. He qualified as a special needs teacher in 1981 and went on to qualify as a Teacher of the Deaf the following year.

I was brought up as a Christian, with staunchly God-fearing Christian parents firmly rooted in the Church of England tradition. We lived in Gloucestershire, where my brother and I enjoyed a country childhood in a very isolated hamlet called Hewelsfield. When I was eight my brother and I attended a mission for children on a holiday, where I committed my life to God. When I was twelve we relocated to Crawley in Sussex. The Church Army Captain of the church we attended held weekly youth Bible study and praise evenings and introduced us to the Pentecostal movement. We also encountered a Youth With A Mission (YWAM) team in Crawley who ran a pizza restaurant called The Cottage Door. A group of us used to spend some of our evenings there, doing more debating than eating pizza.

One lunchtime, when I was seventeen and was sitting in the restaurant with a friend, Corinne, we arranged to go together on a Christian holiday. We both liked the idea of different places, but I agreed to the holiday she wanted, which was a week in a large house in Devon. While we were there, I met a boy called Michael Mednick from Barking. Mick and I kept up a friendly, spasmodic correspondence over the next few years, and would meet up occasionally.

The YWAM team were very welcoming and keen to encourage us in our faith, and they invited us to attend their weekly prayer and praise meetings at their base, Holmsted Manor in Staplefield, Sussex. They would drive us there in their minibus every Saturday and bring us home again. I looked forward to these events, as they were my first real experience of God actually speaking to individuals in words of knowledge and prophecy, and I found them to be very exciting.[1]

Meanwhile, Mick had been discovering a deeper faith for himself. Between the ages fifteen and seventeen he attended similar events in a room above a pub in Seven Kings. There he encountered the teachings of Trevor Dearing, who spoke about the gifts and anointing of the Holy Spirit – that is, the opportunity to give oneself to God more fully and to experience a closer walk with Him on a daily basis. (In the 1970s Trevor Dearing had an apostolic ministry among church leaders; he supported the work of various churches, bringing words of guidance and visionary ideas to them.)

In my teens I became familiar with the music of some emerging Christian rock musicians. Mick introduced me to the music of Randy Stonehill, and another friend

---

[1] A 'word of knowledge' is a term that describes a personal message given by God to someone in a situation such as a meeting where there are others present. It may be, for example, about a pain that someone else might have, which God will then heal through a prayer offered there and then at the meeting. A prophecy is a more general message, perhaps a word picture or a sentence to encourage everyone present. See 1 Corinthians 12:7-11.

introduced me to that of Larry Norman, and at some time I encountered Keith Green, probably through my Cottage Door friends. At school one year we had a visit from Graham Kendrick and Peter Rowe who were promoting their first album, and from that time I listened to as much of this music as I could get hold of. I was learning to play the violin and had not listened to a lot of rock and pop music before this, mainly because I had been involved exclusively in classical music, and I found the lyrics of these artists very challenging.

After I left school I attended Kingston Polytechnic (now Kingston University) to study for a music degree. Throughout our college years Mick and I continued to write to each other and visited each other's parental homes once or twice. The friendship grew into a close relationship when I left university and wanted some help and advice with career choices; I knew that he was involved with children with special needs and at the time I was working in a day centre for what was then called the Spastics Society, having ignominiously failed my degree course.

While at Kingston I settled into a Pentecostal Congregational church in Wimbledon. When I became engaged to Mick I moved to Ilford in East London, near Barking, where he lived and had a secure teaching job; my work at the time was temporary and I had no firm career plans. We searched for a church to be part of, as we knew that the church he had been attending was not right for us. We joined a Pentecostal church in East Ham, which moved to join with a Baptist church in Manor Park in the London Borough of Newham about six months after we joined it. We were married in 1984. We lived in Barking and

Dagenham, the neighbouring borough, but Mick worked in schools in Newham and felt very much at home there.

The beginning

After a few years Mick was asked to serve on the Eldership team of the church, and this he did for fifteen years until we left the Newham church. Those years were very exciting and challenging for us both. Mick had many duties and responsibilities and was heavily involved in the lives of the people in the congregation.

In 2003 we attended a Spring Harvest conference.[2] Mick woke up one night with a very strong impression about uniting churches in local areas, specifically those in Manor Park, in worship and prayer. He said afterwards that it was like a series of instructions, almost like a blueprint, from God. The churches were to work together as His body, to look around the local community and streets and to make a spiritual map of the area. This would involve plotting the churches on a map, and also the temples, mosques, schools, community buildings, hospitals and places serving the public. These places would feature in street praying walks and then in prayer times in which all the churches of the local area would come together. For this purpose, Mick felt God was showing him that the area of Manor Park should be divided into five geographical zones, and the churches would be plotted in each zone. Every year in each zone, three events would be held: a prayer breakfast for the

---

[2] This is an annual Christian conference where attendees can take part in workshops, hear talks and worship God.

leaders, a street praying walk and, a week later, a united churches prayer evening, making fifteen events a year. All three events were to be hosted by or based in a church in each zone, and were open to members of all Manor Park churches, not only the ones whose church happened to be in that particular zone.

In many towns, churches of different denominations regularly meet together to pray for their town, or to support one another in prayer for their specific ministries. Church leaders of different denominations and doctrinal viewpoints have a real closeness and friendship. This is what developed among a group of leaders in Manor Park, and this continued for many years, in the form of the prayer breakfasts. This 'blueprint' would later be used in Barking.

So many of us get up on a Sunday and walk or drive to our church along the same route for years, not ever deviating from a prescribed path or really looking around us at people or places. As we walk or hurry along, the same thoughts may be in our minds Sunday by Sunday. 'I hope I switched the oven on (or off),' or, 'I wonder how Mary is after her operation. I must visit her,' or, 'I hope Mr Jones is preaching today.' We are locked in our own routines and habits and do not often see our community from a fresh viewpoint. Do we notice the faces of the people we pass, or the rubbish in a neglected garden, or the mobility scooter outside number 44? One day I was forced to drive a long way off my usual path because of a traffic diversion, and I passed the local travellers' campsite, a place I knew about but had never actually seen at first hand. As I passed by, I wondered whether anybody thinks to pray for these people.

One of the interesting factors of the street praying walks was the opportunity to walk down roads that we would never normally have a reason to visit unless we knew someone who lived there. We would notice all kinds of interesting little lanes or alleys or community buildings previously unknown.

The whole church united prayer events were held five times a year, involving many churches, and were a combination of worship and prayer, both in small groups and congregational intercession. The five prayer walks would take place a week or so before the planned main meetings, and anything felt to be an issue of concern on those walks and any specific words of knowledge about the area would be noted. These issues would be brought to the main meeting for prayer by the church community. In this way, prayers of intercession would be offered in the prayer meetings for the needs of the people in the local vicinities and the schools and local government and health centres.

These events took place regularly for ten years or more and were times of powerful intercession over the whole of the Manor Park area. Over the course of a year every street would be named in prayer, and the residents of those streets prayed for by small groups. Many people took back to their churches printed sheets of prayer needs, or took them home for personal prayer.

We believe that intercession like this is a powerful opportunity for God to work, as we declare God's peace over the area, asking for His protection over residents and schools and for His favour on the churches. We would ask God to heal the sick and restore broken relationships in the families of the residents. It is important to pray for these things in a potentially volatile community in which people from many different walks of life, faiths and backgrounds live side by side.

Another important God-given inspiration was to arrange outdoor witness events. Mick felt that God was asking him to call the leaders of the local churches to meet for regular prayer events, to do outreach events at Christmas and to arrange monthly open-air events in the town centre of East Ham. Mick approached the manager of the BHS store which was situated on the fringe of the area we wanted to use for our platform, and received permission to use the store's electricity supply for the musicians and PA system. We had a team of musicians and singers from several churches to sing, talk to people about Jesus and pray for needs, and we sometimes had a drama group. We would read Scripture and tell the gospel, but only in short talks.

These monthly open-air events developed into marches of witness at Easter and then at other times of the year, and Mick led a street outreach programme based on the 'Make Way' teaching and ministry of Graham Kendrick. These events were faithfully supported by a core of people; we had a lorry for the musicians and PA equipment and a body of people walking behind the lorry to give out sweets, balloons, etc, carnival-style.

During the last three years of our time in Manor Park I was very unsettled, as I wanted to attend a church fellowship more local to where we were living. I was also working part-time as a violin teacher in schools in Dagenham, which made me feel more involved in the life of the borough we lived in. I was meeting regularly with a teacher in one of the schools in which I taught, to pray for the needs of the school, and I was attending prayer meetings with the mothers of other children in the school my daughters attended. I had attended a local church ever since my schooldays and had continued to do so during my college years, and I wanted to be worshipping in my local community. But I had to wait for the right time. God had not told us to relocate to another church, and I had to trust Him for the future. I was not good at waiting and trusting; I am still an impatient person, many years later, but 'God has not finished with me yet', as the saying goes. There was a lot I had to learn in those years at Manor Park to prepare me for what God had in store for the future.

Part One

The Story

One
The call to Barking

Early Christian influence – a brief outline

This book does not attempt to study the history of Barking and Dagenham, but it is necessary to delve into history, albeit briefly, to see its relevance in the context of prayer and ministry today. In so doing, we are able to discover our spiritual heritage, to see how God has used people in the past and to reclaim in some measure the godly influences that were present in the community over so many years.

Waterways are vitally significant as a source of life, and Barking was established originally near the River Roding. The river was a natural gateway to and from the town, a means of transporting both people and goods, whether for good or evil purposes. It was the river that provided an access point from the sea for the Vikings to invade the town in the eighth and ninth centuries.

The most important historical building in Barking is the Abbey; it is in ruins today, but it was a hugely significant place in the seventh century and beyond. The Abbey was founded in AD 666 by a Christian missionary, Erkenwald. He established another at Chertsey, where he was the presiding Bishop, and his sister, Ethelburga, was the Abbess at Barking, which was an establishment for nuns.

The land granted to the Abbey by the Saxon kings who jointly ruled in Essex encompassed a huge area, and included what is now Barking, Dagenham and Ilford.

In AD 871, following a Viking attack, the nuns from the Abbey fled and were dispersed. The Abbey was re-established in the 900s by King Edgar as a Benedictine convent. After the Norman conquest of 1066, the new King William made a temporary headquarters in Barking before establishing himself in London, staying in the land belonging to the Abbey. The position of Abbess was a very influential one: following the Abbey's establishment as a Royal Foundation, until 1213 all the abbesses were of noble lineage and had royal connections. One of the abbesses was Queen Maud, wife of King Henry I. Another was Queen Mathilda, wife of King Stephen.

As Lord of the Manor, the Abbess had great control over the local population. (This male title may seem strange to us, but this was her official title.) She was responsible for the regulation of weights and measures used in the marketplace. She alone in the Manor of Barking held the rights to grind grain into flour in the Barking watermill. The Abbey housed the manorial court which maintained the roads and bridges and controlled the transfer of lands. The whole social structure of the town was thus under the influence of the Abbey.

The influence of Christianity and the care shown by Christians for the poor and the sick were apparent in those early centuries of the Abbey. The first spiritual duty of the residents of the Abbey was that of prayer. People left gifts to the nuns as payment for prayers and Masses to be said in the event of their death or the death of a loved one.

It is interesting to note that the ministry of prayer has now, as in the days of the Abbey, such a great significance as a prelude to any work God expects His people to accomplish for and through Him.

The Abbess Adelicia established the Hospital Chapel of St Mary and St Thomas of Canterbury in 1145. This was in Ilford and was a hospice for elderly infirm men. Later, the place was opened to lepers. This was the only part of the Abbey to survive after the Dissolution of the Monasteries, and it was eventually converted into an almshouse. It is wonderful to see that, just as society looked to the early Christians of the hospice to take on the task of caring for its outcasts, BCU today has taken on the task of caring for the marginalised, the poor and homeless in Barking.

It is significant that the Christian church at that time was the source of peace and security in the community. When the Abbey fell to the Dissolution in 1539, the nuns were retired with large pensions and the keys of the town were handed to the secular authorities, thus surrendering the church's spiritual authority. Now, more than 400 years later, we believe that God has given a prophetic word that He will take back this spiritual authority and that the spiritual 'keys' to the town will be given back to the church.

Barking's claim to a famous reformer is that of Elizabeth Fry, who was buried there in 1845. The Society of Friends in Barking, otherwise known as the Quakers, was established in Barking around 1658, and in 1672 they bought a plot of land to be used as a burial ground. A Meeting House was established the following year, next to the burial ground, and this became a Quaker centre of prayer and contemplation until 1830.

Elizabeth Fry had a faith in God, and the humanitarian work she did in reforming the terrible conditions in the women's prisons of the time was a pivotal point in the history of social reform. I include her in this account because she embodied the Christian principles of ministering to the destitute and outcasts of society, those who were ignored and marginalised. We have so far briefly mentioned the very sick: lepers, prisoners and criminals, and the homeless. BCU was to establish ministries that would serve a similar group of needy and desperate people. It seems that God's call to His church remains constant, and His people are to champion the cause of the same groups of people.

'Life begins at fifty'

For quite a few months, Mick had been feeling a desire to spread the concept of unity and to extend the vision to other areas, specifically to Barking and Dagenham, our own borough. He did not know the specific time he was to move into Barking; he felt that he should wait until he knew it was an inner prompting from God. My husband is a patient man!

Around the time of Mick's fiftieth birthday, in November 2008, he felt that it was time to prepare to leave the Manor Park churches scene and to start to make our base in Barking. He felt that God had called him to work for unity first, above any work in the day-to-day running of an established church, and that God was telling him that he had to be released from leadership in order to be able to work with many churches without being compelled to be loyal to one. This is a difficult shift in perception, and one that not everyone can understand. A conversation Mick had with a friend and leader, Jonathan Oloyede, sealed this word for Mick, as Jonathan, unaware of the struggle Mick was going through, shared his own experiences about being released by God for a wider ministry.

Another confirmation that it was time to move came from Matthew Porter, a member of Transform Newham, a group of united churches encompassing the whole of Newham. 'If you sit on the fence you will just get splinters,' he said.

The elders at the church we were attending – Manor Park Christian Centre (MPCC) – knew about Mick's calling and recognised that God was orchestrating his departure, and therefore were fully supportive of his call to Barking. By way of transition, for the next twelve months we went to a smaller Manor Park Church where Mick was not to have eldership responsibilities and would work to pass on the Newham baton to a Newham leader and start to meet with the Barking church leaders.

Nearly twenty years earlier we had been friends with Phil and Eunice Burch, a couple from Barking who had also attended the East Ham Church before it merged with the Baptist Church and became MPCC. Not long after the churches merged, Phil and Eunice found a church fellowship in Barking and Phil became a leader there. Our ways parted and we lost contact with them, only meeting them rarely at larger events.

God is so good: He knew that Mick would need a partner in fulfilling the role he felt God was calling him to, and now we renewed the friendship. Mick telephoned Phil and told him what he felt God had been saying, both about his vision and that he felt he would need Phil's help initially in making contact with the Barking church leaders. Phil was in a good position to do this because he was the only remaining contact for a former united churches movement in Barking which had ceased to operate. Phil confirmed this when they met: he told Mick that he felt that this was the time that God would do something new, and that God had brought to his attention two scriptures, one from John's Gospel in which Jesus said, 'Unless a grain of wheat falls to the ground and dies, it remains only a single seed. But if it dies, it produces many seeds.' The second scripture was about new wine needing to be poured into new wineskins, from Mark 2:22.

Phil became a valuable partner and an instigator in establishing the organisation, which would be known as Barking Churches Unite (BCU). Phil is an accountant, and for four years he managed all the accounts and dealt with grant applications and the legalities.

In January 2009 we left the church in Manor Park to start to make contacts within and to network with churches in Barking. We based ourselves at the Elim church, which I had sometimes attended with a friend over the years.

In Manor Park the principal focus of our work with the churches was prayer in the five zones. In Barking, Mick established the same structure as he had in Manor Park, dividing the town on a map into five workable areas and then visiting as many vicars and pastors as he could to explain what the vision was. Some church leaders were very keen to talk; others were at first a little suspicious. Some even said that they had heard what he was doing and had been waiting for his call. God had prepared the way and readied the hearts of those leaders. Mick would share the vision God had given him to work with them to help unite the churches, and he was given many opportunities to attend their Sunday service, sometimes as an opportunity to introduce this idea to the congregation.

This is the prayer zone map Mick devised:

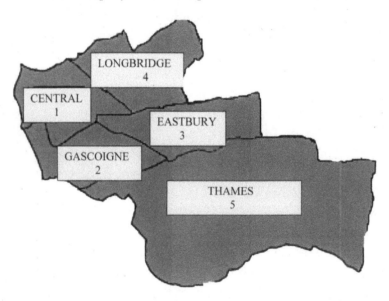

This made very interesting Sundays for us – sometimes we would attend two different church services every week. Until we researched it properly, we had no idea that there were so many churches in the area, both large and small; sometimes as many as three would use the same building on a Sunday. In some churches we were treated like special guests and given the best seats, which was a little unnerving. In the first year the focus was to wait on God and to pray with church leaders every two months on a Saturday morning.

In October 2009 all the leaders came together and agreed on the name, and for Mick to be the coordinator. They decided to hold one street praying session a year in each zone (so five in total), each one to be followed about two weeks later by the united churches' prayer and worship evening This would be hosted by a church from the zone, open for anyone to attend, at which any issues of concern noted on a street praying walk were offered for prayer.

We prayed for the town and for the vision of starting to reach out to the local people. We also prayed for the success of the further development of our partnership as churches. The newly formed trustees were introduced to the church leaders, and the name Barking Churches Unite was officially recognised. The leaders were from the Methodist, Church of England, Baptist, Elim and independent churches of Barking. Now we were an official organisation, and were personally sure that the church leaders were fully supportive of the venture.

A 'prayer canopy' was also established, comprising three church leaders who would be praying about the vision, and especially for Mick. These people would act as an accountability check for Mick, to ensure that his ideas were backed up by the prayer and wisdom of other leaders in his decision-making.

We now wanted to start to put in place plans to establish ministries to work together as united churches in the community. Mick had the support of different church leaders to approach the Council in order to discover what we could do practically to make our presence known as churches and to be of some service to the town. The first project we had in mind was to begin a Saturday children's club. One of the church members had a particular desire and vision to do this, and was keen to get some official backing.

The Olympic Rings picture

Around this time, Mick also devised another diagram, using the Olympic Rings symbol. The image depicted the links from local church work and mission, and moved across the linking rings to the wider community and beyond. Mick explains the significance of the picture here:

> This picture was given to me just after Barking Churches Unite was formally established in 2009 and was also given to a number of other people I connected with at the time. The picture was a strategy to take a nation for Jesus. Each ring signifies a practical way to reach people but relies on the unity of the churches to accomplish it. The first ring signifies local churches (zones and small areas) working closely together. The second ring links together with the first and third rings in that this model is then duplicated across a borough or county. The third ring signifies a whole borough or county seeing what neighbouring areas are doing, learning from them and working with them to bring about a similar model to bring

about transformation. The fourth ring then duplicates this model to a regional context (North West England, North East England, Central England, South East England, London, South West England) The fifth and final ring signifies regions working together to capture a nation for Jesus.

Another word of guidance came from Jane Holloway, the leader of the National Prayer Network. She had been working to unite church leaders in different localities to pray and work together for mission. Mick contacted her to explain the vision of the Olympic Rings and its connection with his desire to unite churches. She affirmed his calling, saying that other people had felt they had received a similar picture of the Olympic Rings. Six months later she came to Barking to see what had been going on and to hear about the prayer networks.

Questions for reflection

1. Have you researched the significant historical Christian influences in your town?

2. How might this spiritual tradition be an inspiration for us today?

3. Has God singled out an apostle in your area to coordinate church unity? If not, pray for someone with this gifting to come forward.

Two
Prayer is the key

We have encountered the power of God made available by God in the prayers of ordinary people because of their desire to unite. When leaders and members of churches of completely different denominations come together, putting aside personal or church agendas to prioritise prayer, God blesses in abundance.

> How good and pleasant it is
> when God's people live together in unity!
> It is like precious oil poured on the head,
> running down on the beard,
> running down on Aaron's beard,
> down on the collar of his robe.
> It is as if the dew of Hermon
> were falling on Mount Zion.
> For there the Lord bestows his blessing,
> even life for evermore.
> *Psalm 133:1-3*

Prayer is fundamentally the most valuable tool we have been given by God; without it, any efforts to start community ministries are in vain. How many churches of different denominations in one town meet together regularly to pray for each other's needs and mission? How many of their leaders have a real closeness with each other? With prayer, this was achieved in Manor Park; it evolved over the years, encompassing leaders with different doctrinal viewpoints and priorities but with the common aim of preaching the Christian gospel.

The plan

'You haven't got time to stand around drinking tea,' Mick said, half in jest. 'I have lots to tell you. God woke me up last night and has given me a plan.'

I became fully alert. History seemed to be repeating itself; it reminded me of the time God had woken Mick during the Spring Harvest conference week. I sighed. This was supposed to be a day when we were to visit our daughter at Nottingham Trent University. Now it was turning into a whole 'something else', and I had no idea what we were letting ourselves in for. It was probably going to be something huge that would take a large chunk of our time and energy. But it sounded exciting, and if God had woken Mick up again, this was REAL, and we were privileged to be included in God's plan.

'Write a list of spheres of influence in the community,' he said as we sped along the M11. 'Social care, children and youth work, education, politics…'

'Mick, this is ridiculous. You want me to write what looks some kind of budget plan for the Council.'

'I know, but this is the stuff that God gave me last night and we need to organise it.'

'Does this have to be done right now?' I complained. I had been looking forward to a comparatively restful day out with Mick and our daughter, Catherine. But yes, it did, my inexorable husband urged. So we brainstormed ideas in the car.

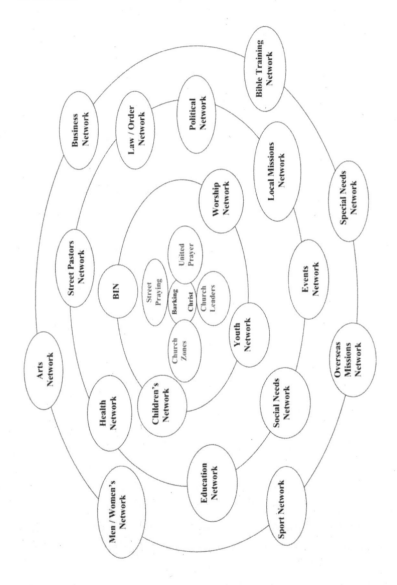

A few days later Mick had produced a diagram which was then stuck to our kitchen wall for about two years. He called it the 'planets' chart. It had what seemed to be an impossibly unrealistic list of what he called 'spheres of influence', many areas of life in which it would be wonderful to see God at work.

After fourteen months, I noted in my diary, the inner ring networks of the diagram had been established.

Street praying

Five times a year we go street praying, or prayer walking, in each of the five zones of Barking in turn. This venture is not for the faint-hearted, as it can involve up to two hours on a Saturday, and we go out in all weathers. It has been interesting to see that from a personal perspective I thought I was familiar with the town I have lived in for thirty years, but the street-praying routes have taken me down streets I have never walked before and enabled me to see new areas. Even walking along a street I think I'm familiar with because I often drive down it can throw new light on an area because it is seen from a different perspective.

Sometimes we discover hidden features of a place: a hidden garden or a beautiful tree, or an aspect of a waterway otherwise hidden from the road. We also sometimes see hidden things that God reveals, or someone may be given a scripture by God. In addition, on these walks we have opportunities to talk with members of other churches we may not have otherwise met informally. Although we are there primarily to pray silently as we walk and together when we stop, there are plenty of moments for a quick chat too.

In walking around an area like this we look for signs that might give us any spiritual insight into the area. Many are obvious, such as litter in the streets or a well-kept garden, a house with a key-box outside and a ramp, indicating the presence of an elderly person.

Sometimes God gives one of the walkers a message or a special insight into the condition of some area or estate, and these form part of our prayer strategy in the united prayer times a week or so later. There may be a particular sign on a wall, or a street name such as King's Street or Angel Way, or a sudden break in the clouds or the unexpected illumination of a feature, which might be seen as a sign of God's goodness or favour. The discovery of a rundown, apparently derelict, pub called The Hope was an opportunity to pray for new hope and purpose and social cohesion in the community.

Every year the routes we walk are changed slightly so that we walk round a different set of streets within the same zone, always starting and finishing at a designated church. Mick puts a map on a board outside the church with the route highlighted in yellow so that any latecomers can find us. As we walk, we stop outside or near significant sites such as schools or doctors' surgeries or the MP's office, and one of us will pray for the work there. We always pray with our eyes open, and we pray silently as we walk, not out loud.

Sometimes we have an opportunity to tell people what we are doing; for example, if anyone enters or exits the place where we are. Sometimes we can even pray for individuals. We have never encountered hostility, and most people are pleased to hear what we are doing, if surprised. On one walk we found a new hostel for the homeless and were able to pray for a man standing just outside after he told us his story. Another time we were in a residential area and a pregnant Asian lady approached us to ask the way to the Children and Family Centre. One of our walkers offered to walk there with her. On the way she found out that the lady was alone, with no family in the country except her husband, who had not accompanied her, even though he had promised, to the Centre. It transpired that she felt lonely and afraid of the whole process of pregnancy and birth. Our prayer walker was able to pray with her and communicate a sense of God's peace to her; the lady consequently felt much comforted.

Sometimes on our walks we have noticed what we know to be a local signal to drug dealers of a location to buy and sell supplies. We have prayed over this issue and the problem has moved away from the area; though, sadly, they have, in all probability, simply moved elsewhere.

The BIN

Another prayer group that we established was a small number of intercessors drawn from different churches to meet together informally in our home. This group would pray specifically for leaders over issues too sensitive to be made known in a more public prayer meeting; for example, health problems. We would also pray for local community issues. As they were established, we prayed for specific BCU ministries and continue to do so. Over a period of time this has become a close-knit, but by no means exclusive, group of about seven and is affectionately known as the BIN – the Barking Intercessors' Network. The picture here is self-explanatory: we put symbolic rubbish in the bin to clean up the streets through intercessory prayer.

The first gathering of the BIN was in November 2009, and since then we have met nine times a year. We pray not so much for the needs of particular churches but for the community; we look at the local newspaper and pray for schools, local events and any particular problems we are aware of in the community. Christian action and community projects should be first prepared and then supported by prayer and, conversely, some prayers need their 'shoes on' to be effective. (If we are praying at home we are often 'wearing our slippers', rather than our 'outdoor shoes', ready for walking or working.)

What good is it, my brothers and sisters, if someone claims to have faith but has no deeds? Can such faith save them? Suppose a brother or sister is without clothes and daily food. If one of you says to them, 'Go in peace; keep warm and well fed,' but does nothing about their physical needs, what good is it? In the same way, faith by itself, if it is not accompanied by action, is dead.
James 2:14-17

The intercessors in a town are the spiritual watchmen and women, keeping guard over the residents. A well-known acronym is PUSH: 'Pray Until Something Happens'.

There are just seven members of the BIN, in spite of my efforts to increase the numbers in the early days. These seven come from four different Barking churches. Each prayer time generally starts with thirty minutes of chat and catching up as well as talking through the issues for prayer. A lot of laughter generally precedes the serious business, and we have occasionally taken people home at nearly midnight.

We especially bring before God the whole plan for unity among the church leaders and we pray for those leaders: their work, their health and their vision. God has been gracious to give individual BIN members particular verses from Scripture, or someone may receive a vision (a picture or an impression), or a word of knowledge and encouragement for others in these meetings. All these are particular gifts of the Holy Spirit mentioned in the Bible in 1 Corinthians, which some of our intercessors have.

The advantage of hosting a smaller group in one's home is having the freedom to spend the allocated time freely with no agenda. I do write a few subjects on notes and place them on our noticeboard, but we do not always include all of them, because God may sometimes lead our prayers in a different direction. We can then focus our prayers on this item and pray in a more concentrated way. At each meeting we review the noticeboard to see what God has changed since we last prayed together.

The WIN

A BCU music network was early on established as part of the prayer network, called the Worship Intercessory Network (WIN). This was to be not so much a formal choir but a gathering together of people who lead worship in their churches, an opportunity to share songs with each other, to share music-making skills and, above all, to pray for one another.

The group members would encourage each other to be open to God's leading in their services and in the worship ministry in the united prayer meetings, and other events that may occur. Like the BIN, this group has become a close-knit group of friends who have been guided clearly by God about what He is and will be doing through His people in Barking.

United prayer meetings

The united prayer meetings are, of course, more formal. A time of worship is led by the worship team of the host church or another church, and then we have a specific agenda, involving praying all together or in small groups. As well as opportunities to pray out loud, we always have a time of silence, in which we wait for God to speak, maybe through a prophetic word or a scripture.

You may be wondering how we address the issue of encompassing different styles of worship and prayer to suit people from different traditions. We do this by using many different formats of prayer in our meetings. There are times of quiet reflection for private prayer. There are invitations for anyone to speak out any perceived prophetic words. The songs and hymns we use are from a mixture of resources, so that there is something that everyone can identify with, as far as this is possible. We also pray in different ways: small groups praying together, in pairs, or corporately with everyone being led from the front.

We pray specifically during these meetings for issues in the zone of the church that is hosting the meeting. Subjects might be prayer for the local schools, the local police community officers, local government, the residents, and so on. This is always a continuation of the street praying session which happens a week before the meeting. On the prayer walk, intercessors sometimes receive a picture or a word from God about the area or a specific need in the street; these issues are then taken to God in prayer at the meeting. Once we invited a policeman to tell us about gang warfare in a particular area and we were able to pray for him and his colleagues.

The pastors and ministers of the churches in the host zone are always prayed for specifically. I well remember one such occasion when we felt the blessing of God on the churches of the area. Various people received specific words of encouragement for the ministers present, and I remember thinking how lovely it was that a teenage girl from the Baptist church was praying for a Pentecostal minister, and an elderly Anglican lady was praying with the Baptist minister and his wife.

The only 'downside' of the preparation for these evenings is the inevitable need for PA equipment to suit all the different buildings we meet in. We considered that it would be less complicated for BCU to purchase some equipment of its own. But where was it to be stored? My diary in October 2011 contains a rather despairing entry mourning the lack of space in our house; many more projects were happening by then, and it was not just PA equipment that we were storing.

An area of known drug trafficking in Barking has gone, and the atmosphere in a school which had some discipline issues changed in the weeks after we began to pray for the staff and pupils. Someone in a local church was approached by someone connected with the school, because they had heard rumours that we were praying for the school. The church member confirmed that this was so. The person then said something like, 'Well, in the last few weeks the children are behaving much better and a Christian Union has been started.'

At the time of writing we have not yet established groups of prayer warriors in or for particular schools.[3] (I

---

[3] 'Prayer warrior' is a term often used to describe someone who will spend a long or an intensive period of time praying about a

wonder, if we were to establish a Schools Intercessory Network, what its moniker would be: the SIN? This does not seem quite suitable, somehow!)

When my daughters were young, a group of local mothers used to meet monthly to pray for the school our children attended. We would pray for the teachers, any known difficulties in the school and for protection for the children, and we know that this was a valuable thing to do and that it had spiritual consequences. (We believe that God honours our prayers and that He listens and will act on our behalf if we pray in line with His will.) In its own way, this was a small forerunner of the prayer networks in BCU, as we all attended churches in Barking.

The prayer diary

The monthly prayer diary was devised by Mick and is given out regularly to churches for the benefit of those who cannot attend meetings and want to stay in touch with what we are doing. They also serve as a general reminder of the various ministries, the churches and their workers who are in need of regular prayer. In the diary we include a BCU ministry every day, a church and its leader, perhaps a school or a location in the borough, or a local public service. Many people value this as a tool for prayer. (For a sample prayer diary page, see Appendix 1.)

---

certain issue, until they feel that God has given them a 'closure' on the matter, that He is answering the prayer.

Questions for reflection

1. Have you ever walked around your town with a view to being open to impressions from God?

2. Do you know what the difficult social issues are in your town? For example, are there known areas of drug dealing? Are there areas where young people always congregate? Are there housing estates with a high proportion of elderly residents?

3. Would it be useful to form a cross-denominational intercessory group?

4. If you hold united prayer meetings, do you pray for issues affecting your town? Do you pray for ministries that churches share? Are there times of silence when you wait for God to speak?

5. Would a cross-churches worship intercessory group be something to consider?

Three
Links with the Council

The Council

Now that the prayer initiatives had been established, Mick felt emboldened to approach the events organiser in the Council to explain that we as churches would like to offer to contribute to the community by organising some public events. In October 2010 he suggested that perhaps the Council would like to provide us with an opportunity for a children's choir to be staged in the town centre near Christmas to sing carols to passers-by. We would also tell people the Christmas story and could give out sweets. The reply was positive, and we were offered a space outside the library, just off the main market thoroughfare.

The Christmas open-air event duly took place, in the enclosed area near the library. It was led by the newly formed WIN. The event included musical items by a choir of children from four churches. This was very popular, and the programme of traditional carols and the children's slot were repeated. We had members handing out mince pies and invitations to the Christmas services in the churches all over the town. It was very cold but the children acquitted themselves well. People always smile when they see children performing, and that day was no exception.

It was now February 2011. This was God's time. Mick absolutely knew that God wanted the Christians in Barking to have more influence in the borough and to be a force for good. The most obvious way to do this would be to approach the Council, to find out what gaps there were in their social and community provision and to see whether the church could offer to fill these gaps, even in a small way. Mick also knew that the months leading up to the Olympics in East London in 2012 would be a potentially significant time, as the Council may be open to ideas to bring people together to engage in some way with the whole Olympics event.

Project or ministry?

Before continuing, it would be helpful to explain the difference between our use of the terms 'project' and 'ministry'. In the first two years we referred to our work as community 'projects'. Then we changed the label to community 'ministries', because this is a Christian concept. To minister is to serve, and this is what we intended to do, bringing the love of Jesus to our town. The term 'project' seemed to us, by contrast, rather secular and corporate.

In order for the church or a group of churches to have any impact in a town in the field of community work or ministry, it is necessary for them to be accessible and open in their plans, and to be seen to be working towards the good of the residents, not simply 'feathering their own nests'. The most impressive community projects in the eyes of the Council authorities, or 'community ministries', as we prefer to call them, would surely be those that meet a present need, perhaps something the Council would like to see take place but have no way of funding.

In order for our witness to be most effective, we should be looking for gaps in the social care network, perhaps opening a youth centre on church premises because funding for the Council-run one has been withdrawn. There may be a need for a lunch club for the elderly for the same reason. If the churches can come forward in this way and offer their services for nothing, this can be a very powerful statement about God's love for the people in the town.

In February 2011, Mick and I were able to attend a meeting with some of the Council members to explain what we as churches wanted to do in the community. We told them about the children's club that was being planned and about our ideas for Companions (see below), and perhaps a hospital visiting service and a separate volunteer service to operate in the community They were especially interested in the idea of Companions, as there was currently a gap in the Council and voluntary sector provision for this work.

Companions was an idea to gather a team of volunteers to regularly visit housebound elderly people. There are many such people in the borough who do not see anyone during the whole week, except perhaps the meals-on-wheels service provider or their health visitor.

Of course, we had to reassure the Council that, although we are a faith-based organisation, we would not treat people of other faiths differently and we would comply with all the discrimination and other relevant laws. I was concerned that my husband was becoming a little carried away at this meeting, and I was wary of him making promises we could not as yet fulfil. However, looking back, the meeting was very productive because it showed the Council members present that we as churches are interested in our local community and want to help its vulnerable members.

'The church has never been interested in helping the community before now,' commented a Council member. Mick replied that he was sorry that the churches had not been proactive, but now we wanted to work together as a group of churches of different denominations to demonstrate God's love in the community. This would comprise members drawn from the Methodist, Church of England, Baptist and Pentecostal churches, and any other Christian church members who wished to be involved.

An indirect result of this meeting was that Mick received a phone call from the events organiser of the Council in March. She had received positive feedback about our small open-air event at Christmas and wanted us to do a performance at the Dagenham Town Show in July and to enter a float in the Barking Carnival. She was very interested in the idea of the churches joining together, although if it had been one church wanting to promote itself, she would not have been interested.

Looking back on this phone call some years later, I am astonished at how unusual this was. Surely God was at work here. How often does a Council events organiser think of approaching local churches to take part in a major Council festival or other event? This was the beginning of a relationship between the Council and BCU that was to last for several years and was epitomised by an ongoing dialogue between Mick and the leader of the Council. He (the leader) could see the potential of using the willingness of church members in the borough to fulfil some functions in the area to help disadvantaged people.

One Borough Day

The Dagenham Town Show in July 2011 and other Council-organised events, such as the One Borough Day, a publicity opportunity for local charity and Council-run organisations, would for the next few years provide opportunities for the churches to raise their profile in the community and for the local Christians to have a voice and an impact in the borough as a force for good. This would be our first opportunity to join other community groups at a borough event. Although this kind of event may not have been to everyone's taste, it certainly gave us a presence at a public event. There were some doubts among us as to whether the whole thing would be possible; the church music group that had agreed to provide the background worship music for our float were very much delayed and did not arrive until a few minutes before the whole procession of carnival lorries was about to leave the first park. They then had to load all their equipment and instruments onto the lorry while attempting to keep it dry in the steady rain which had just started. I remember climbing onto the back of the lorry-float and having to literally hold the keyboard steady so that our keyboard player could play while it rocked around as we went along! In the event, our float was the only one with live musicians – I am not sure whether we deserved an accolade for this fact or whether it was just a bit mad, considering the weather!

The faithfulness of the church members who came to join the procession in the pouring rain was rewarded by a positive report in the local newspaper in which the churches' float was mentioned along with those belonging to the other organisations, and by many happy faces at our marquee, which hosted the only professional magician. Many people came to our tent just to escape the rain, and they were given some of the gospel message and offered prayer if they needed it.

Questions for reflection

1. Are you aware of any gaps in Council-provided social care in your area? Do you read the local newspaper to find out what goes on in your town?

2. If you work in a church-run facility, do you look upon it as a project or as a ministry?

3. Can you form any links with your Council?

Four
The early ministries among children

After two years of holding prayer gatherings of the various kinds it was time to launch our first BCU ministry: a Saturday morning children's club called Kidz Klub.[4]

This came about when Mick received a word from God to approach two people, Muriel and Suzanne, in two different churches about starting a children's club. They had both received a similar word from God but had been told to wait until someone approached them about doing this. When Mick spoke to them, it was confirmation that they should undertake the leadership of this venture.

The organisation, administration and financing of this ministry were huge, and were undertaken by Muriel, a lady with a passion for work among children. Suzanne would take on the planning of each session of the club. At least a year was needed for preparation – this would happen throughout 2010 – and a lot of prayer support. The club would not be opening until March 2011. Both Muriel and Suzanne knew that this was God's ministry for them and they were still passionate about it four years later.

---

[4] This is also the official name of an established organisation, and the name is used with permission.

Muriel knew this ministry was close to God's heart. She says the planning, although spread over a long time, went very smoothly with no major obstacles. (This is not always the case when we want to set up a Christian ministry, however, because there is sometimes opposition.) She felt it right to approach the local schools, and the first one she contacted agreed to be the host building for the club. This in itself was significant for two reasons. Firstly, this particular school had not been particularly open to any Christian involvement or influence in the past. Secondly, this school in Barking town centre is the largest primary school in the country at the time of writing, and is surrounded by a huge estate of high-rise flats. What a wonderful opportunity this location presents for the spreading of the gospel and the teaching about God's love to the local families.

There was a certain amount of equipment to buy for the club. The money for this came mainly through grants that Muriel applied for. One of the last items on her list was a cheap but durable carpet for the club. God said one day to Muriel, 'Don't worry, I have many carpets for you somewhere.'

The next day she and Mick were driving around, looking for discount carpet stores. After a disappointing visit to Manor Park, where the place they were hoping to visit had unexpectedly closed down, Mick felt they should call into a branch of a well-known carpet chain in Barking.

'Do you have any samples or offcuts available?' he asked.

The manager took them to the back of the store, where there were more than a thousand carpet squares. 'We have a lot of them. We are closing the store and need to get rid of all these.'

That evening when Mick came home, he said to me, 'I've got a little job for you. Can you help?'

I braced myself. I knew from experience what these 'little jobs' usually entailed.

The following Saturday afternoon, three of us transported literally hundreds of carpet squares from the store to a container near a church that was going to send a load of them to Africa, and a large pile of them came to our house, where they were temporarily stacked to the ceiling in our loft conversion. It was exhausting, and took us four hours and twelve car-loads. But we were very happy; God had given us all these carpet squares for nothing.

God had provided exactly what the club needed. Squares of carpet are much easier to transport and store than a bulky roll, and three years later they were still in good condition.

The Barking Kidz Klub opened in October 2011. It was BCU's first successful ministry, and it is still flourishing. The club operates for one hour every Saturday and caters for children aged seven to eleven. When I visited the club three years later there were about thirty children, mostly from the local housing estate. A typical morning consists of an opening game while the children assemble – a sack race was the chosen game that particular morning. Then they sing some Bible-based, fast-paced songs, with lyrics that speak of God's power or goodness. A team game with buckets and beanbags, welly-racing and a Bible story followed, in which some of the older children were invited to act out the story as it unfolded. There was then an opportunity to talk about the story, which was about Jesus calming the storm and walking on the water, and an opportunity for the children to pray. The session ended with another sack race before the children were collected by parents.

The children and families speak very highly of the club and the host school has allowed it to be promoted in a small way. Word of mouth is, of course, the most efficient means of recruiting members, as the children tell their friends about the club.

A small group of older children are official helpers, with their own uniform T-shirts. This is a testimony to the success of the club, as they did not want to leave it when they became officially too old. One of these young helpers is from a family who moved to Dagenham, and he still comes across the borough to be a helper.

Some children have found the club to be a source of constancy during an unsettled time at home when their parents are going through relationship problems, for example. For the majority of these children, the club is the only organised activity that they can access; opportunities for weekly dancing or sport activities are not common for the children living on this estate.

For Muriel and Suzanne, the joy of running the club is to see the children drawing closer to Jesus, having an opportunity to hear about and to pray to Jesus, and for Him to reveal His plans for them. They believe that God has a purpose and destiny for each child and they want the children to discover this for themselves. Children have just as much potential to be used by God to bring words or prophecies as do adults, believes Suzanne. Some churches do not recognise this, and do not give children the opportunities they need to flourish and to discover their spiritual potential. At the club they learn how to be secure in God's love, how important it is to forgive in their relationships with friends and family, how to be kind, and many other important life lessons. Children have grown in confidence, some have changed their behaviour patterns, and for some their relationships with their parents have improved. Many parents have expressed deep appreciation for the club, and the club leaders have sometimes been able to pray with parents about troublesome issues.

One aspect of the Kidz Klub ministry is the midweek follow-up visits to each family to say hello to the children. During one such visit the team discovered that the children did not possess a proper bed, only a mattress on the floor. This affected the children's sleeping patterns and their performance at school. The following week the team members' church had a collection and bought bunk beds for the three children and a rug for the lounge. The parents were blown away by their generosity. This is the kind of opportunity for sharing God's love in the community that the Kidz Klub provides.

Suzanne shared with me that the work has deepened her faith, in small everyday ways. She told me that the week they opened there were lots of children and three helpers – and there was 'no riot'! Somehow, in spite of the occasional lack of team members available for a session, the work always gets done and the atmosphere is positive and calm; often a team member who was not on the rota will turn up. Muriel says that the planning and delivery of the

Bible lesson helps her in her walk with God, reminding her of an attribute of His love.

In early 2018 the club relocated to a church the other side of Barking. This is because the school raised its rental charge. Many of the children still come all the way from the housing estate, and the host church is opening up a lounge facility for the parents and offering tea and cake. It is a lovely opportunity for church members to build relationships with the families.

The Music Academy

This is our second community ministry and was originally conceived to help to give some musical training to budding musicians, from both the churches and the local community, at a comparatively low cost. They would receive musical instrument tuition and teaching about the rudiments of music-making. Our local Council-run Saturday music school had for many years been providing training in the playing of orchestral instruments; we were not trying to compete with this provision, but were specifically offering help to church musicians and others in the playing of keyboard, guitar and drums.

Lessons were offered to adults and children alike, but our main students were children, who could have lessons at less than the current going rate by learning in a group. We invited local music teachers who were experienced in their field and glad of the extra work on a Saturday morning. We were unexpectedly given some keyboards by a local school and we received a private grant in order to buy other instruments to start up.

It was October 2011 and a busy time for us personally because the Kidz Klub and the Music Academy, as well as a third initiative – a food bank – had all been lined up to start around the same time.

I include an excerpt from my diary from this time:

12th October 2011

As I look around the house I am in despair. As soon as we get rid of anything, something else comes in. For months now we have had various bits of PA equipment being delivered, and boxes of stuff for the Kidz Klub. Dennis and Pam (next door) have been very kind about taking postal deliveries in when we are out. The whole of the downstairs toilet area is stacked with PA stuff which has to be hauled in and out for every prayer meeting, and some Kidz Klub equipment which comes out every Saturday.

The box room is piled high with carpet squares and some kind of folding tables for Kidz Klub. We have three guitars and a large keyboard standing against the back of the sofa and Mick has just left the house to go to buy a drum kit – and I know just how much room they take up!

The Food Bank opened this week and we have bags of food which have been donated from the Harvest Festival services of several churches in a corner of the living room…

Fortunately, I am not a house-proud sort of person, but even I found the chaos we lived in for that short time extremely difficult. To add to the general muddle, we also had some extra things in the house from Mick's father's flat. He had died in October 2010 but we did not clear out his flat for some months afterwards. We took the time and trouble to salvage his large stamp collection in the belief that it would be valuable to someone. This was in huge boxes, stashed upstairs.

One of the Barking churches meets in a large warehouse facility and offered to house the Music Academy. We offered lessons in keyboard, drums, singing and guitar, in groups of five or six for a whole hour. In spite of some practical problems that sometimes occurred as a result of the building being shared between us and the church, the Academy ran successfully there for a whole academic year, and we were able to give a concert in the summer term to showcase the children's newly acquired skills. The church was very pleased to see the progress of the children concerned. However, it decided after a year that its involvement with us was no longer a priority, so we parted company, and we found an alternative location for the next academic year.

We have been fortunate to have very good instrumental tutors, and the opportunity for people from all the churches in the borough to gain some proper understanding of music-making is invaluable. Some families would not have been able to afford instrumental tuition for individual children; these lessons are much more affordable. The Council-run Saturday music school has now ceased to operate owing to cutbacks, but our Music Academy is still running, and serves a need, providing we can still operate from a church-based venue.

It was a difficult few months, as so much was happening at once after we had spent much time praying about opening these ministries in Barking. We had been given a lot of money from an organisation that supports churches working together in local mission, and were able to start all these ministries at around the same time. At first we were given some temporary storage space in churches for some of the equipment, and we were able to hire a storage unit for a short time, until the Council gave us a facility for the Kidz Klub equipment.

Food Bank

The Food Bank had recently been started by a leader of one of the local churches. Mick had been involved with some of the planning, in order to help the project get established and to help the leader facilitate the ministry. Over the years it has become a vital ministry and is now a charity in its own right. It operates from a building that the Council has designated for this purpose, and the Council offers financial support for the ministry by paying rent and electricity. The building also hosts the church that the Food Bank manager leads.

Questions for reflection

1. Is there a local Council-run facility that has closed owing to lack of funds? Could your church members step into the gap?

2. If the gap is a big one, could you be praying with other church leaders and members about the possibility of joining together to provide a service?

3. Does your community have a Food Bank? If not, could one be established?

Five
The Vicarage Field connection and YWAM mission opportunity

Our local indoor shopping centre, Vicarage Field, has a huge Christmas tree in the middle of the main precinct for the whole of December. This has unexpectedly provided a wonderful witness opportunity which has often been talked about for months afterwards.

The Christmas tree must be the most exciting and 'successful' venture of the first three years of BCU. It all started when Mick spoke to the director of the shopping centre, Simon Green, about the possibility of carol singing around the tree and about future initiatives to help the people of Barking. Simon offered the tree to the churches for the month of December 2011, and he suggested it as a memorial tree. Mick immediately said we would call it a prayer and memorial tree. People would be able to write out prayers on cardboard stars and place them on the tree and would be able to receive prayer if they wished.

Simon also said that he would invite Mick back after Christmas for a chat about how he could offer future support.

We had no idea what we were embarking on. We had to provide stars made of gold or silver card – and lots of them. We called on the services of a handful of kind friends who committed to cutting out and threading with ribbon bags of stars at a time. December is a busy time, and we were asking them to use free time they probably did not have. We ended up producing and using more than a thousand stars – way beyond our expectations. Of course, we had to find volunteers for this venture; we were asking people from churches to commit to standing at the tree for two or three hours at a time in the busiest period of the year when they already had so much else to do.

A timetable of volunteers was duly formed. Pairs from different churches manned the stall by the tree, offering shoppers the chance to write a prayer or a loved one's name on a star. Some shoppers responded with enthusiasm, some were dismissive, some were curious. We all found the task extremely interesting; surprisingly, many people had no idea what prayer is, and we were able to explain the concept of a God who actually cares about them and is interested in their welfare and is available to call upon at any time.

'What shall I write on the star?' was a typical question.

'Anything you like,' I would reply. 'What would you like God to do for you this year? Or how about thanking God for something?'

'How about thanking God for your parents?' said Phil, my partner for the session.

We had an opportunity through this event to collect money for our ministries; this kind of thing often produces a response by people wanting to give something.

'What are you collecting for?' was frequently asked. However, we had decided at the beginning of the venture that people should not be paying for prayer, so we always refused. But we did have a large plastic bin by the side of the table and we invited people to give to the Food Bank, if they wished to.

What a privilege it was to talk with these people and what great needs many of them expressed. Jesus would have been there at that tree, in the shopping centre, making Himself available to talk and pray with everyone. Some people, when they realised they had been given the opportunity, wrote very personal and heart-rending needs on the stars. Perhaps it was the first time some people had ever asked God for help. It was an even greater privilege to be able to pray with some individuals and to be able to offer them a word from God or share a passage of the Bible.

The whole venture was a great success and Simon Green was very enthusiastic. He called Mick to invite him to a meeting early one evening. Mick went in some trepidation.

'I have been watching your people at the tree and I am so moved,' said Simon. 'I saw an Asian lady give a tiny baby to an old lady to be prayed for. Surely this is the real spirit of Christmas, like baby Jesus.' That particular event was rather special: the baby had been on her first outing and her mother wanted prayer for her. We obtained her permission to record this special event in a diary. The reason we did this was so that certain people on the team (who are often called 'prayer warriors') could take these people's needs on their hearts for a short period of time afterwards and bring them to God in private prayer.

The response by the public to the Christmas tree witness was wonderful. The response by some churches was, sadly, not so enthusiastic; it is a big commitment at a busy time of the year. But all the church members who took part in the venture said how much they had valued it; it added a new dimension to the whole Christmas experience and they were excited about next year.

As a direct result of this successful time, Simon offered us a space in a shop unit on the top floor of the shopping centre, shared with the Disability Advice Shop. By now he had seen that Mick had a passion for people, and good organisational skills, and they were building a mutual respect.

We were really thrilled; this would give us a definite presence in the town. We would be visible to the public and able to use one side of the shop window to advertise our services such as the Kidz Klub and the Music Academy. We would be allocated a desk space, a cupboard and a filing cabinet, and would have a small area in the shop allocated to the disability group. An added bonus was that Muriel, our BCU administrator and Kidz Klub project leader, would be able to work there instead of in our house, which would be better for her and for us. Some of the ever-growing pile of equipment for the projects could also be moved from our house to the shop.

The shared shop space was a great blessing for the next eighteen months, until May 2012. We at last had a space in a public place. Sharing premises with another organisation brought its challenges, but we really appreciated the opportunity. We were very thankful and wanted to honour God in this, and to be seen to use the place respectfully and maintain a good working partnership with the other occupants of the shop. We would have liked larger premises, but perhaps this was a stepping stone. This proved to be the case, as a few months later God released a new space for us.

'Megacities'

The latter part of 2011 had been a very busy time for us. The Music Academy had started, producing a lot of administration, and the Food Bank and Kidz Klub and, as if this were not enough, on 10th October I looked on the calendar to see what we were doing the following week.

'What's this on the calendar, Mick? It says, "Megacities Meal 2 pm".'

'Oh, that,' he answered, guiltily.

'Do you mean people are coming here for a meal, or you are out for dinner, or what?'

'It's a meal here.'

'Oh, and I've got to cook for ten people or something?'

'Erm, well, yes, actually.'

'And when were you going to tell me this news?'

'Well, I put it on the calendar.'

Megacities is an initiative run by the Youth With A Mission (YWAM) centre in Perth, Australia.[5] Teams of up to twenty young people are sent to a major city where they stay for six weeks or more, and every alternate year a different city is chosen. Several teams are sent to different parts of that city during the year and they do evangelistic outreach, street praying, run children's clubs and generally get involved in whatever evangelism effort their host church is carrying out. This dinner was to be the setting for a planning meeting with two visitors to discuss the

---

[5] YWAM is a global mission organisation which runs evangelism courses and discipleship courses, providing opportunities for people to travel the world and take part in missions of several weeks. Perth is one of its bases.

possibility of a team coming to work with us in January 2012.

We were very privileged to have three teams during the year staying in different areas of the borough for two months each. The Olympics was, of course, a major factor in their choice of London for this year.

The first team arrived between Christmas 2011 and the New Year. Unfortunately for the team, it was extremely cold; they had been in Perth, so the change of temperature was difficult for them. They were staying in a church hall, kindly made available by the Barking United Reformed Church, which is a small congregation of elderly people. The YWAM team were in their late twenties or older. They duly arrived at our house with all their bags, straight from the airport. They all seemed to be incredibly tall and their luggage filled the room, until we suggested it all went outside on the patio. Inevitably there was a delay in their projected arrival time, causing me some anxiety about keeping food hot for twelve. I had prepared a roast chicken dinner, as it had seemed to be the easiest option.

What generous and open-hearted young people they were, this group of random strangers from Switzerland, Australia, America, London, Holland and Germany. Of course, they had been together for the three-month YWAM School in Perth, so they all knew each other pretty well.

The team based themselves at the church and were able to use the church kitchen to cook their meals, and they had time in the evenings to meet together and to talk and pray over what they had been doing.

The principle ministry the team were able to work in was helping in the Kidz Klub on Saturdays. They also began a process of 'spiritual mapping' of the town. This involved walking and praying in the streets, and noting on a street map the position of mosques, Hindu temples, churches, community buildings, medical centres, public houses, schools, and so on. The team also recorded where there were piles of rubbish, heaps of empty drink bottles or evidence of drug-taking (needles and other paraphernalia). In this way, potential problem areas in the town could be spotted and especially prayed for in our united prayer times.

While they were with us, the YWAM team spent much of their time walking the streets of Barking and talking to people, one to one. They did a lot of street praying. The first thing they did, though, when they moved in to the church hall was to take a few days to read the whole Bible out loud, in shifts of two or three, day and night until completed. This is YWAM policy, and they believe that the spoken Word of God has great power over the spiritual forces in any town or city. Every YWAM team that stayed in the borough began their time in this way.

I have since wondered why we as churches do not adopt this policy, even in a small way. In fact, since spending time with the teams, Mick has instituted four 'Read the Bible in Barking Days' a year, when we gather in one of four churches in turn in four different months to do this very thing over a six-hour period, broken down into drop-in time slots, on a Saturday. This has proved to be hugely rewarding for those who attend, and we are gradually working our way through both Old and New Testaments, continuing each day where we left off the previous time. The first year we ran the Day, a pastor of one of the churches encouraged families in his congregation to join in, and he reported that the children found the experience of reading aloud very enjoyable – and they had been reading Leviticus! We were very impressed!

Once the reading was complete, the YWAM team started to walk and pray round the streets, talking to anyone they could about faith, questioning what people thought about God and praying for needs. They also helped in a weekly church youth club, for which the vicar was very grateful, as he had been struggling to staff the evenings.

The work of this first Megacities team was not as clearly defined as for the subsequent teams, as there were no large community outreach or other events scheduled for that time of the year. A good prayer foundation had to be laid for the events planned for later in the year to coincide with the Queen's Diamond Jubilee and the Olympics. When the first team left us, they brought their time to a conclusion by hosting a supper where they shared a report of their experiences and passed on particular prophetic words they felt they had received for the area.

The second team arrived in time to help organise a planned outreach event to commemorate the Queen's Diamond Jubilee. This was to be a series of barbecues held simultaneously in various locations of the community on a Sunday. We had some professional help from an organisation that came the day before to help set everything up.

This second team were of a younger age range than the first, and needed a little more supervision and care, as well as help to negotiate transport and planning time for travel, cooking, and so on. They also stayed in the United Reformed Church building.

After they left, we were told that we were not to be given a third team, much to our disappointment. However, the day after we were told this, God said to Mick, 'You need to prepare for a new Megacities team; you are going to receive a phone call.'

Mick was taken aback. 'But we have nowhere to house them.' The United Reformed Church was not able to take a third team on.

'Trust Me,' Mick had the impression that God was saying.

Sure enough, the call came through, and we were to choose between a team of twelve or a team of twenty. Mick accepted the smaller team but he still did not have a living space for them. What an exercise of faith... he had about five hours to find somewhere and confirm with the team organisers.

At the last minute a large church in Dagenham opened its doors and we were off again, and this time the team were able to centre themselves in a completely different part of the borough, which was a blessing to the church and to the residents of a new area.

The third team arrived in May; this group were here for several large outreach events, including a united churches witness for the arrival of the Olympic Torch as it arrived in the borough, and a united churches event, called God in the Park, in July. This was a large festival weekend where local worship groups and Christian artists, musicians, puppetry and drama groups were able to present the gospel and perform in a local park. This event had been planned for several months by a Dagenham church. The Megacities team were invaluable in their support of this venture, providing help with carrying heavy equipment, manning stalls, providing refreshments, talking to people, and so on. Unfortunately, the weather turned against us and it rained heavily for most of the weekend. In spite of this, the event was considered to be a definite success: it established a precedent for future events and united the churches across the three neighbouring boroughs to come together to provide a witness.

A wonderful opportunity arose in the lead-up to the Olympics. The manager of the Dagenham Town Show telephoned Mick and requested members of churches to be standing on the roadsides, demonstrating a presence and perhaps making some music on the Sunday morning the Olympic Torch was to arrive in the borough. The event was to be televised and he wanted people in the community to be out in full force. We were invited to literally take our worship on to the street. The Torch Relay was to be combined with the annual procession and Dagenham Town Show which immediately followed, and we were able to put together a carnival float representing the united churches across the borough.

We chose to display the theme 'Children of God', in keeping with the general carnival theme, and to our surprise our float won the prize for the best float – an added bonus. It was wonderful to see everyone come out of their houses and cheer us as we had a lively band of musicians on the carnival float, gathered from several churches.

The gathering of Christians for the Torch Relay was a great success. We had people from different churches playing in live bands at three places along the route where the Torch would pass, and we also provided refreshments

for the onlookers and face-painting for the children. One of the local pubs kindly provided us with a power supply and even gave food to the band members. To date we had not joined with the local Catholic churches for any event, but now we were able to use the power supply from St Thomas More Church for the musicians stationed outside. We also had face-painting stands outside the church and balloons for the children. Once again, this was a great opportunity for 'the church' to be seen by the public in a positive light, and we made the most of it.

At the end of the academic year, in July, we shared a meal with the last Megacities team and they gave us some feedback from their experiences here. They had some very challenging observations, the first of which was that they had found the youth of the borough to be quite open to chatting about spiritual issues when approached on the streets and in the parks by members of the team. This, we were told, was an open window of opportunity.

One of the spiritual strategies of YWAM is to enter a park and pray, to ask for God's presence to come, and to worship there. This draws people, out of curiosity. The second observation by the team was that we need to make people in the churches aware of the scope of opportunities for witness and evangelism in the community. Young people are especially open and asking questions, and many have a wrong perception of God.

(I have since realised that the Megacities team found young people especially open to the gospel probably because they were the age group primarily approached, being closer to the age of the team members. Other age groups are also seeking the truth.)

The third point was that people need to be invited to events or to our homes in friendship; people will not readily walk into a church. People will be drawn to what they see in us if the presence and love of Jesus is manifest in our lives.

A very key point brought by the team was the constant need for unity among churches; this is the only way that God will pour His richest blessing on the borough. 'There is a great divide: Barking and Dagenham,' observed one of the team. 'It should be Barking–Dagenham with no "and" to divide.' This statement was the one that really stuck in our minds as we bade farewell to the team. We later called our night shelter, when it was set up, Hope 4 Barking–Dagenham. The churches in the borough, and indeed in the whole country, need to work more together. There are too many divisions of tradition, denomination and race. These need to be overcome in order that we can receive God's full empowering and full growth.

The UK, said the team, has been used by God to bring God's blessing to the world, and some of that anointing is still here. They said they believe that God will do something here that will have repercussions elsewhere in the world.

When I consider that statement now, it seems a huge claim, and I wonder how this could come about. Then I think of the work of all the Christians which has taken place here in Barking down the centuries and I am sure that our work, just as theirs was, is part of God's larger plan for the furtherance of His gospel to the nation.

We need more stars!

At the end of the year it was time to repeat the Christmas tree witness in Vicarage Field shopping centre. This time the tree was even more popular than it had been the previous year.

Two thousand stars were placed, in spite of the fact that we were not there for very long: the early morning times could not be covered owing to a lack of volunteers. We quickly exhausted our supply of card stars and had to recruit some voluntary help from some church members to make more in the evenings.

The witness at the tree was beginning to grow by reputation, and some people remembered us from the previous year. Mick and I attended a wedding in December where a friend told us that she had been having her nails done in a beauty parlour near the tree and the beautician recommended that she go and see the people at the tree to be prayed for.

One thing that we had omitted to do the first year was to organise ongoing prayer for the people who wrote stars, except for a few particular people who requested it. This second year, we took the stars off the tree and gave them out in bags to intercessors who wished to pray again over the needs. Even if someone prays for that need once only or prays for the child who wrote, 'I want a PlayStation for Christmas,' God will work some good in the life of that individual.

Questions for reflection

1. Does your town have a Christmas tree every year? Pray about the possibility of an opportunity for a Christian witness there.

2. Have you made any links with the director of the local shopping centre?

3. Spiritual mapping – do you know the location of the local spiritualist centre, mosques or temples? Can you pray with others about the influence of these places?

4. Have you ever considered speaking the Bible aloud in a concentrated period of time, such as a whole morning, or reading it in this way in your town?

Six
A year of preparation

A wonderful surprise

We were now based in the Disability Advice Shop unit in Vicarage Field shopping centre. Sharing a working space with another organisation is not ideal, and there were some difficulties.

One morning in May 2013, when Mick was praying, he felt that God was telling him to make an appointment to see Simon Green, the director of Vicarage Field, to tell him about the work that God was intending to do in the shopping centre through BCU, and then to ask him a question: 'How can you help us?'

This was a really bold move for Mick, but he was absolutely sure that this was God's instruction for him.

Simon was keen to see Mick immediately, as he had been wanting to see him too. Mick's first thoughts were that there might be some kind of problem. However, at the meeting Mick did what God had instructed him to do. He shared what God had done over the past two years and his dreams for the future: to be able to have a space where people could come to be given help or advice, and how he knew that the people in the churches could offer their services to run more community services. He then followed this with the question, 'How can you help us?'

Simon replied, 'I can see your heart for the community and how much you do to help people in Barking, and I can also see that you are professional and do things well. What you really need is a shop.'

Mick replied, 'Yes, that is what we need, but we couldn't afford the rent!'

Simon asked, 'Well, can you afford £1 per month, £12 a year?'

'Yes,' replied Mick.

'So it shall be. I will give you a shop for twelve months and then let's see how you get on. I will contact you in the next few weeks with a shop for you.'

Mick was astounded; he had obeyed God's leading to go to see Simon, with no idea or expectations of what would occur in the meeting. He phoned Phil Burch immediately afterwards. 'I can't believe what just happened. We have just been given a shop!' What an incredible God we worship.

We were so excited that this provision had come from seemingly nowhere. God really was bestowing His favour on Barking and our efforts. The idea for the shop was not to sell anything material, but to 'sell' Jesus and His love to passers-by. It would be a place where people could come for prayer, for a chat, like they did at the Christmas tree, and to find out about BCU's community projects, or ministries, as we were now calling them. They would also be signposted to services in the borough, such as advice shops, playgroups, health centres and other related services, such as youth services.

A prayer team was duly formed, along with a small team of people who would take the vision to heart and design the space. The idea was to make it a unique space where the people coming in would feel the presence of something special; it would be a place of calm and purpose where they would feel able to talk about anything in confidence. We knew that this opportunity would really give us a chance to introduce people to Jesus. We did not have long to wait; God had in mind a specific time to unveil His plan. In October we were given the promised unit.

It was truly to be an exciting few months of planning and preparation. We did not know that God would be giving people many ideas and strategies, putting things in place and stirring the hearts of both Christians and others outside the church in order to accomplish His purposes.

The night shelter: joining the dots

One Sunday morning in May 2013 Mick woke up and said that he felt that the Lord had told him to contact three church leaders and to say to them that God intended for a night shelter to be started in Barking and Dagenham. 'I need to phone Pastor Emmanuel right now,' he said.

The call was made, and Emmanuel said that he had been waiting for Mick to call, as the Lord had woken him up a few days before saying he should start a night shelter and that this would be affirmed by Mick. He had lost Mick's phone number and was waiting for a call from Mick in the belief that God would help him renew the contact. He asked Mick to go to see him straight away, which Mick did. The upshot of the meeting was that both Mick and

Emmanuel had received a word from God that a night shelter was needed in the community. They had both had this issue on their minds for some time.

The building where Emmanuel's church met was a warehouse, where there would be plenty of space to house people and to prepare food. Pastor Emmanuel asked what the next step should be. Mick replied that they needed to contact the other two people in accordance with God's instruction. Mick was unable to contact the other two people because of the busyness of the day. However, that evening we went to an open-air concert in Barking Abbey ruins. At this event Mick saw Steven, the second person he was to contact. They saw each other from a distance and hurried towards each other.

Mick greeted Steven, saying, 'God has told me something.'

'I know,' replied Steven. 'I've been anxious to see you. God has told me we need to start up a night shelter.'

Mick was able to confirm this and told Steven about his meeting with Pastor Emmanuel that morning. Steven also asked what the next step was, and again Mick said that he should contact the third person first before going forward.

A few days later Mick contacted the third person, Graham, who also stated that he felt he should be involved in starting a night shelter. After speaking with Graham, Mick felt that a meeting between all four should take place. What an amazing story this is to the glory of God. All four people met a week later to pray and decide what to do next. Within the prayer time at that meeting there was a feeling that they needed to find out who else God might have spoken to in the borough. It was agreed that Mick would send out an email to all the church leaders in Barking and Dagenham to find out.

Within twelve hours of sending the email, Mick received a phone call from a Church of England vicar, Julie, who said that she needed to see him urgently. When Mick went to see her, all the leaders of her church were present. At that meeting she told Mick that God had told her a year earlier to have a shower room and new toilets installed in the church building. She knew they would be needed for a night shelter. The email was an answer to her prayer and obedience to God. What an amazing God we serve.

The preparation

A committee was formed over the following weeks, consisting of interested church leaders. It was nine months of hard work and planning to open the Hope 4 Barking–Dagenham night shelter, and there were plenty of problems and obstacles to overcome. A venture of this kind is a colossal undertaking, with many legal implications and red tape. Additionally, lots of money is needed to even start up, let alone to operate. The biggest expense was to pay someone to be a watchman to stay awake all night; some of the church leaders, not to mention the insurance company, were unwilling to have the premises and guests unguarded all night. All the other staff would be volunteers from different churches who would come and clear the floor space if necessary, cook supper, clear up or prepare breakfast. The guests would be referred to us from the Council and would have been vetted by the police.

Finding equipment

Once the night shelter had been publicised, other organisations and people became interested. Out of the blue, we received a car full of soap, towels and bedding from someone who knew one of Mick's work colleagues.

From May to December that year the time was full of preparations and prayer times for the two committee groups setting up and preparing both the shop unit premises for our proposed ministry to the disadvantaged, and the night shelter. They had to make numerous phone calls, check the legal requirements for the planned ministries and promote the plans among congregations to find potential volunteers. The BCU united prayer meetings were excellent forums for this. The BIN was another important regular meeting where the plans were all prayed through and laid before God.

We had some difficulty finding churches that were willing to host the night shelter. There were volunteers from churches to cook and clean but we needed venues across the borough. The church with the warehouse was able to accommodate four nights a week, which left three over the weekend. Churches were reluctant to open their buildings on a Saturday because of the Sunday services, in spite of our promises that we would be out of the building before 9 am. Eventually we had enough places to be able to accommodate our guests for the whole week.

At a BIN meeting, one of the members said he could drive a trailer and would take on the task of finding one on the internet. This would be necessary for the transport of bedding and essential equipment between venues. A large food wholesaler had promised free food which would otherwise be wasted. This would be collected twice a week, which meant that we had to install refrigerators in the shop unit. It also meant that the cooks had to be inventive and willing to cook whatever had been provided.

We had been hoping to start in November, but we finally opened the night shelter in February. Admittedly this was towards the end of the winter period, but at last we had opened. The ministry was named Hope 4 Barking–Dagenham (H4BD).

Elf and safety!

In 2013, the Christmas tree witness hit what we at first thought was an insurmountable obstacle. Concerns about health and safety had been raised: there was a fire risk in placing hundreds of cardboard stars on to a tree that was hung with electric lights. It looked as if we were to be prevented from operating this year, and we received the news with a mixture of sadness and annoyance. We asked the intercessors to pray. If God wanted this to take place He had to move, and fast. It was already mid-November.

After some negotiations with the management of the shopping centre, a compromise was reached. The large Christmas tree on the ground floor was not to be used by us; it would be the property of Santa and the elves. But we could station ourselves next to the less-frequented upstairs grotto area which consisted of a display on a small platform. Now we had a problem: with no actual tree, how were we to attract people to our station to pray? 'Place a prayer star on our noticeboard' did not have a very Christmassy or attractive ring to it…

We were told that the answer was to have a tree, rather ironically, made out of wood or chipboard; this would be something the management could sanction, and of course it would be ours to use as often as we liked. So, a very obliging engineer/draughtsman called Keith drew up plans overnight, and within a week we had a tree made by the Vicarage Field shopping centre maintenance team. This in itself was an amazing intervention by God, saving us a lot of time and money and proving that the centre was fully supportive of our mission. Once the wooden tree was painted it looked very impressive.

Once again, we need not have worried about the response from the public. In spite of not being situated in such a busy public area as the previous two years, we had a constant flow of shoppers coming to see what we were all about and we were able to pray with many people. God will always find a way. By the end of day five, our only concern was whether our new tree would be large enough to hold all the stars.

Two people became Christians at the tree that year, in spite of us spending less time there during the daytimes. God was granting His favour on the work.

Some lovely stories have arisen from the Christmas tree witness. A group of ladies from a Church of England in Barking have a ministry of being able to give words of knowledge when praying for strangers, imparting a sense of God's presence or peace to the person. Their leader is a lady called Lorraine White, who also runs a monthly quiet day for ladies in the churches. Lorraine was at the tree one day, and a lady approached her and asked for prayer. Lorraine duly prayed for her and for her unborn child. Most surprised, the lady told Lorraine that she had only just found out that she was pregnant. Lorraine told her that she felt God was telling her that she would have a boy. Sure enough, in Easter week the same lady came to see Lorraine. (We had been given an opportunity to hold a similar witness opportunity in Vicarage Field for the weekend.) The lady was able to confirm that yes, she was expecting a boy, and she was overjoyed and amazed that God was interested in her.

2013 had been a year of preparation. We had waited to hear about our promised shop unit. The night shelter preparation was well under way. The regular prayer times had been continuing, with the united prayer meetings being attended by a number of regulars. The BIN had continued, with the core of seven regular intercessors, and, of course, the street praying walks on Saturday mornings continued. God was preparing the people for a new spate of activity in the town; exciting developments were ahead.

For a leaflet detailing basic advice for potential Christmas tree witness volunteers, see Appendix 2.

Questions for reflection

1. When do you need to wait on God for preparation and prayer and direction?

2. Have you heard God speak to confirm the right time to begin a ministry?

Seven
Ministering to the homeless

The year 2014 proved to be a very significant and exciting one. Our two major mission opportunities started operating concurrently: in January we were preparing to open our new shop unit in Vicarage Field shopping centre, and the night shelter in February. The two ministries have to date been our largest and most significant, and were very integrated at first, The Source (the name of the shop unit) being used as a base by the homeless people who were from there referred to the night shelter.

The name 'The Source' is taken from the concept of Jesus as the 'source of our salvation' from Hebrews 5:9: 'He became the source of eternal salvation for all who obey him.'

In March 2014 we were almost ready to open our new shop premises. A group of us spent some days in the weeks leading up to Christmas 2013 painting walls and cleaning. It is wonderful how God provides for His work by supplying help from unexpected places. We needed adequate flooring for the shop and had no money. Miraculously, some free carpet tiles were found by searching on the internet. Now we had to find transport for them and someone to fit them.

Mick told the caretaker of the school where he worked about the carpet tiles, and he recommended a lady who was experienced in carpet-fitting. This young woman was very interested in the story of what we wanted to do with the shop and wanted to give something to the community in her time over Christmas. Quite unexpectedly for us, she volunteered to lay all the carpet tiles, with her friend, free of charge. We were completely astounded at her generosity, especially at such a busy time of the year.

The final stage of preparation was taken over by a 'home-grown' design team of women from across the churches. They designed the layout to include a reception area with seating, a separate closed-off prayer space, and a back wall covered in cascading white-and-blue chiffon to represent the flowing of God's holy river depicted in Revelation. Quiet Christian music would be playing in the background, and the atmosphere would be peaceful and welcoming.

There would be a separate office area at the back, with space for three desks, where it was planned that people from the Kidz Klub or from BCU would be able to hot-desk from time to time.

The Source has been through many changes and different focuses over the years. In the first few months it literally became a refuge for a young homeless man called Albert who had been staying around Vicarage Field shopping centre during the day, and the security people knew him well. Albert was from Ghana and felt he could not go home, although his time in the UK as a student had ended, as there was a rift between him and his family. For the first year of The Source being open Albert was almost a permanent 'resident' during the day. He came to regard Frances, our part-time manager at the time, as a mother figure, and she looked after him, supplying him with food and drink, warmth and friendship. We were quite concerned that he was drifting through life with no apparent purpose, but eventually one of the staff members at The Source managed to discover that Albert had an aunt in London. We were able to contact her and reunite them. Albert eventually returned to Ghana, relationships repaired.

The Source became a focal point for the night shelter clients for a while during the shelter's second winter season. This was a development that we had not anticipated, and it did cause a few problems. Guests would come to The Source and sit there for several hours a day, creating a less-than-professional atmosphere. Eventually we had to ask them to restrict their visits to set hours in the week.

One day the police brought a woman and her child to The Source. She had been shoplifting in the supermarket on the floor downstairs. If we could not help her, they said, she would have to be arrested and taken to the police station, and they did not want to do that. She had been stealing food for her children. Frances gave them something to eat and some vouchers for the Food Bank. She also gave her some food to take home from the Food Drive collection for the Food Bank that was happening in the supermarket that day. It turned out that the lady was victim of an unscrupulous landlord. The Source referred her to a housing agency and within a few days she had been given permanent accommodation elsewhere.

Easter outreach

The success of The Source in those first months and the popularity of the Christmas tree witness emboldened Mick to ask Simon Green whether we could run a similar kind of witness event over the Easter weekend in 2014. To Mick's joy, Simon said we could run an Easter Saturday concert at the display area on the top floor opposite The Source.

We asked various church leaders if they wanted to take the opportunity to hold a one-hour witness slot. They could bring some musicians to perform some praise songs and give out hot cross buns and tracts about the Easter message, and perhaps invite people to their services.

The all-afternoon, free concert was very popular that first year. We ran it for about four hours. Four churches signed up to perform for an allocated time-slot. During the last hour the church music group had to make room for a short while on the stage for the Vicarage Field Easter Bunny, who joined in the music-making and raised a few laughs from the onlookers. It was great to have the opportunity to tell people about Jesus in a public place at Easter.

The night shelter; the visible poor among us

Meanwhile, the development of the night shelter ministry had been an exciting and, for Mick, an all-consuming venture. It had to be thought about and planned, with many meetings and telephone calls to church leaders and to potential volunteers, without whom nothing could be done. People were needed to open up the church, to drive the trailer containing all the cooking equipment and bedding from the previous night's venue to the present one, to fetch food from our supplier and then from the storage facilities at The Source, to cook the food, to spend time there in the evenings befriending the guests, to sleep overnight and finally to clear up and to lock the premises after breakfast.

It seemed like an enormous undertaking, but God supplied all the people we needed to manage every process.

I include here an entry from my diary which contemplates the contrast of my comfortable circumstances with those of a homeless person.

1st June 2014
Today I awoke in my nice warm bed, having enjoyed a sleep in a secure place with my wonderful husband. I had a hot shower and dressed in clean clothes. I prepared my food before going out and, looking around me, I sit in a warm kitchen and eat off clean plates. I have a job to go to and yesterday I paid money for comfortable new shoes.

In stark contrast to my own comfortable situation, there are many homeless people in Barking, and we can only imagine how difficult their lives are, especially in cold weather. It was only during the time I worked at the night shelter and later at The Source that I began to have any inkling of the plight of these people.

Why do I refer to 'the visible poor'? These people are without hope, mostly without any employment, without a permanent residence; some are sellers of *The Big Issue*.[6] They stand on street corners asking for help; they are very visible, if only we would take the time to notice them and speak to them. They try to shelter from the rain in shop doorways at night. They sleep on park benches. They even sleep in the church graveyard.

The 'invisible poor' I would consider to be those behind locked doors, those who are forced to choose between heating their homes and buying food for their children. Many people in our inner cities are in desperate financial situations, yet we are unaware of their difficult circumstances.

It is to the poor in general that God wants us to minister His love and grace. He has a special place in His heart for the poor: people of all types and backgrounds, those in self-made situations and those who are the victims of circumstances beyond their control. At The Source we are able to help both of these groups of people.

Homelessness is a grim reality in Britain today, one which is often forgotten. Councils have no money to spare for rough sleepers, and the common perception tends to be that these people have chosen a life on the streets to avoid taking part in society or paying taxes. They are not perceived as respectable.

Living in Barking, I am made aware every day of the plight of the homeless. There are usually people begging on the streets in the town and around places like the railway station, where people sleep in doorways.

---

[6] *The Big Issue* is a magazine that offers 'employment opportunities to people in poverty'. For more information, see https://www.bigissue.com/about/ (accessed 23rd October 2018).

Homeless people are to be found all around London. One particular kind of begging is particularly dangerous: at a traffic light junction on the A13 there are to be found one or two individuals begging from the drivers of stopped cars, constantly putting their lives in danger in the road. One man I see frequently; he limps slowly, as one foot is held awkwardly to one side, thus making it impossible for him to move quickly in case of danger. These people are truly desperate, yet we as society have become desensitised to their needs.

Homelessness is possibly the worst kind of poverty. People are victims of unscrupulous landlords who hike up rents, or of those who hire out tiny rooms for large prices. Others might be victims of domestic violence which causes them to flee their homes. Some have lost their jobs owing to eviction; some suffer with mental illness. They may have broken relationships, and sometimes they might temporarily lose their benefits. These homeless are very ordinary people, like you and me, who have fallen on hard times; they are not a strange breed of people to be avoided.

Hospitality

The word 'hospitable' is defined in Webster's Dictionary as 'gladly and generously receiving guests and attending to their needs and comfort'. The words 'gladly and generously' are particularly challenging, as they should both be present in a true spirit of hospitality. It is not enough to give hospitality grudgingly or out of a sense of duty; this is ungracious and unloving. Unfortunately, this is what sometimes happens if we are feeling duty-bound to offer a bed or a meal but are under a lot of stress in our work life, for example, or are under some time pressure to complete a job. The true sacrifice is to give willingly and joyfully. So often when we serve someone in spite of our own needs, we find we are very blessed in return. We serve a compassionate God who calls us to be Christlike.

Serving in a night shelter is an easy and safe way of offering hospitality to complete strangers whom we otherwise would not consider inviting into our home. The time we spend with them is determined by us: how much time we will give and on what day; even the type of work we are prepared to do, whether it be kitchen-based or relating one to one in conversation or prayer.

Jesus Himself was a traveller during His ministry, with 'nowhere to lay his head' (Matthew 8:20). He 'went through all the towns and villages' (Matthew 9:35) and 'went through the cornfields' (Matthew 12:1). We frequently see phrases in the Gospels like 'going on from there' or 'entering the place' (or town). Jesus and His disciples were constantly in need of hospitality.

Joining up more dots: the night shelter in operation

A committee was set up, with Mick as the Chair. The original overall operation of the night shelter ministry was taken on by the pastor of one of the churches and his wife, whom God had been using to run a soup kitchen in another church in the borough, a building they borrowed from yet another church. Their work in the soup kitchen turned out to be a good preparation for the night shelter ministry, and when they had to relocate their church they transferred the ministry to The Source. They were our first 'operations managers'. The night shelter initially ran for one season of three months and then had to close, owing to lack of funds. During that time the Council housing department, the police, The Source and the churches all referred guests to the night shelter.

The vision for the project was not only to offer a night's accommodation to the guests but also to help them into the housing and the benefits system. This is a huge undertaking, and we had a church leader who took on the responsibility of working with the guests and the relevant agencies.

When I first visited the night shelter, the guests were cheerfully helping to unload the trailer and bring in the beds, someone was starting to prepare vegetables and the tea urn was heating up. There were seventeen guests that night, two over our official limit, and the food would have to stretch. I was working in the kitchen. A couple of young women in their twenties had been working almost every night they could, because they really loved the work. A lot of banter and laughter issued from the kitchen, along with some good-natured disagreement concerning how much chilli should be added to the mince. There was a friendly atmosphere, music was playing, people were playing board games or dozing in chairs.

I talked to George, one of the guests. He had been sleeping at Victoria Station where the foxes would come to bite his face and fingers. He also suffered from rashes on his face from constant exposure to the elements.

That first season we were able to accommodate twenty-three guests who stayed more than twenty-eight days. (The twenty-three were not all there together; that is the number we accommodated during the whole season.) Twelve of these men we managed to help obtain benefits and two gained employment. Nine were allocated permanent accommodation. Being associated with BCU and coming regularly to The Source meant that the guests could use The Source as their permanent address in order to get into the benefit system. (It is supremely ironic that in order for a homeless person to be given any chance of gaining benefits or, indeed, to be allocated any accommodation, they need an address!)

That first season we were a given an award by Housing Justice – a national Christian organisation for supporting the homeless. Apparently, these figures are very unusual; we attribute our success to the grace and glory of God.

As mentioned, after three months the night shelter was forced to close owing to lack of funds. All the guests were upset about this, but they understood the reasons. We naively asked some of them if they were less bothered about sleeping rough over the summer. They told us that they are sometimes more vulnerable during the warmer months because other people are on the streets later at night, increasing the risk of harassment.

On the final evening we held a barbecue for the staff and the guests. Over Easter, Mick and I had been privileged to attend a concert given by a choir in Brentwood, at which a speaker, Terry, gave testimony about how God had rescued him from a life of crime and homelessness. His story is a very powerful one and Mick invited him to speak at our barbecue. Terry duly came, with a friend, and was so impressed by the atmosphere and the whole place that he later offered to bring the Brentwood choir to Barking in the autumn to perform two concerts to raise money for the night shelter. We were overwhelmed when he also told us that some people in his church were willing to give funds to us as well.

The concerts duly took place in September 2014 in St Elisabeth's Church in Dagenham. We were advised by the choir leader not to sell tickets but to take up a collection at the end, as this would raise more money. To our surprise, this proved to be the case.

The choir was a really professional-sounding one, and produced a high-quality gospel sound. On both nights the church was full and the local Mayor and Council leader were present. Three of our night shelter guests shared their stories.

One other member of the Council was present: a Christian lady who had her own story of how attendance at St Elisabeth's Church had helped her in her own spiritual walk. It turned out that the concert was at the very church she had attended as a little girl. She had later wandered away from her faith in God until one day she passed St Elisabeth's Church and read the sign, 'Jesus is the Light of the World'. This spoke into her heart and led her to want to attend the church in Brentwood where she was then living. This lovely lady worked for the Council to promote voluntary groups, and she subsequently became involved in helping Hope 4 Barking–Dagenham apply to become a charity and, later, BCU. How amazing it is that God joins up the dots in ways that we cannot imagine.

The guests

In that first season we were able to accommodate fifteen guests at a time in the shelter. We ran the night shelter initially for three days: Friday to Sunday. All the guests had had police checks and had been referred to us by other agencies. They were predominantly male.

Our first lady guest was Janet, who attended the shelter with her husband, Richard. They were a Christian couple in their sixties, originally from Canning Town. They soon established themselves as very much at home in the night shelter. They loved to help in the kitchen and they were friendly with everyone. They soon built a close friendship with a young man with learning difficulties, who arrived in care of the police one night. When Richard and Janet were rehoused in permanent accommodation at the end of the season, they asked for this young man to be housed nearby so that they could keep an eye on him. In the following night shelter season all three of them came several times a week from Tilbury on the train to the night shelter venues to help out, and they became valued members of the team. Without them we would have been very short-staffed on many evenings.

Richard and Janet: their story

Like many others, Richard and Janet came to be made homeless because their landlord raised the rent. After spending a few nights with family and then in a hotel, which they could not afford, they went to the police for advice, but the police could not find them a long-term answer.

After about two weeks their church leader put them in touch with our night shelter. Five weeks later they were allocated a flat in Tilbury, through the efforts of the volunteers at The Source responsible for rehousing guests. Soon Richard and Janet became fully involved in all the areas of the ministry to the homeless, helping out not only night after night but also in the daytime, volunteering at The Source. They got to know all the night shelter guests and felt valued members of the community. Richard and Janet have found a new sense of self-worth. 'People treat you with respect here,' they said.

They helped get the food together at The Source, pushing trolley-loads of cakes from there to the church across the road. They cooked, slept overnight and listened to the guests' personal stories. Because they have spent time on the streets themselves, they can identify with the guests, some of whom look on Janet as a motherly figure.

'The night shelter really gives you a picture of what people have to go through. It breaks your heart,' said Richard. He told me that after a long time working there, they have built relationships with the guests and 'the barriers come down and you see the other side'. He believes that God made them homeless for this reason: to give them a job to do and a really satisfying ministry.

He also says that the whole experience has deepened their faith in and reliance on God: 'When you are really down, God always steps in and helps you up.'

Ironically, Richard and Janet spent on average only two nights a week in their new home during the night shelter season, because they wanted to be serving the homeless.

'Some people ask us if we get paid to work there. But it's a far greater reward than money,' he said. 'We are doing what God wants us to do, and you can't beat that.'

The only thing they dislike about their role is the heartbreak of sometimes having to turn people away because of a lack of space. 'Another thing we don't like to say is, "We are going home now."'

The winter season, 2014

The following winter we were not able to open the night shelter until November 2014. This was because we needed to plan our financial resources. BCU was not able to apply for charity status at this time, which meant that the usual financial resources were not open to us. (It was not until June 2017 that we finally achieved this goal.)

The operations manager and his wife resigned after a few weeks, and Mick became responsible for the running of the night shelter and of BCU as well as having a full-time job.

Opening in November, of course, meant that for the first time we would have to consider what we would be able to do about Christmas. I include a piece from my diary at this point:

I am writing this on Christmas Eve and Mick and I have spent the last week visiting night shelter venues and organising rotas, transport of food and investigating church kitchens for equipment. Mick has been out for hours, doing more of the same, and I am at home, waiting for his return. I could feel annoyed and frustrated by this, as we have been so busy, but then I make a call to my friend Paula who is also alone a large part of today, because her husband is now waiting for several hours in hospital for treatment for his cancer. I know in which situation I would rather be.

Organising a night shelter for Christmas Day and Boxing Day poses a new set of problems, one being the lack of volunteers, and another being the lack of public transport to get volunteers home after a long shift, or even to the venue beforehand. The volunteers had to be willing to drive or use taxis, which is not possible for everyone.

We were fortunate because another group, who were helping the Havering night shelter, had cooked a meal for us for Christmas Eve, and we had a large amount of extra food from our supplier. Each guest had a Christmas dinner and a wrapped gift, and they could stay at the shelter all day.

One of the guests was a seasoned veteran of the streets. He was a Christian who would normally be in a church service on Christmas Eve and New Year's Eve. He told us that he had at first been disappointed not to have been able to attend a watchnight service, but the next day he realised that he had, in fact, spent all of the night in a church (although it was a church hall), and he had been able to be alone in a side room to spend a long time in prayer, which had been a real blessing.

In this second season we sheltered two young women, both of whom had fled their homes: one to avoid an arranged marriage. The other girl was in a similar situation: her parents disapproved of her boyfriend and she had run away to live near him. This young woman suffered from seizures, had been diagnosed as having a brain tumour, and needed, on occasion, to be admitted to hospital. Many people are homeless because of a rift in marriage or family relationships.

Making a commitment to working at the night shelter weekly or fortnightly for the whole season of six months is not easy. For the cook, it is a very unpredictable task. We don't know what food will be available until we arrive, or sometimes what kitchen equipment will be there. Because we are a mobile organisation and have to move everything every night, some things inevitably get mislaid. I take my own supplies sometimes as a backup. The cook needs to be very creative with tinned meat and pasta. Some weeks we have a lot of fresh vegetables and fruit. Other weeks we have to use frozen vegetables, and we always have a lot of baked goods: buns, scones and cakes. There is always enough food for everyone, helpers included, even though sometimes the meat has to be carefully shared out. Cooking dinner for fifteen people from an unpredictable supply of ingredients in a strange and often ill-equipped kitchen is something I would never in my wildest dreams have considered volunteering to do a few years ago, but as I have been involved in the work it has become easier. My friends would laugh at the idea of me doing this; I am not the most organised person at home. But God always helps us in the tasks he sets before us. Somehow the task is achievable from sheer necessity, and I know that however the food turns out the guests will be very grateful, and we have had some really nice meals.

One Saturday I was standing in the tiny kitchen of our smallest venue staring at a pile of ingredients, thinking, 'What exactly am I going to do with this lot?' I really was struggling to feel enthusiastic.

Then in came a beautiful Caribbean lady, Joy, who said, 'I am here to cook. You can go and talk to the guests.' I was so relieved. God had helped me again, and the meal she created from pasta, tinned meat and some vegetables was both imaginative and delicious. It turned out that Joy was a professional cook, and she helped out at the night shelter quite regularly, in spite of having three children and an elderly parent to care for.

Every time I cook at the night shelter, I am struck again by the sheer wastage of food by the companies who supply us; we use merely a small proportion of what gets thrown away each day. We sometimes have to jettison some of what we have ourselves at the end of the evening, perhaps fruit that is too far past its sell-by date, but at least we are stopping a small part of the waste by using it in this way.

Charitable status

In spring 2015, Hope 4 Barking–Dagenham became a charity in its own right. This meant that the food and resources received for The Source had to be kept separate from those of the night shelter. It was two more years before BCU itself became a charity, and this came about because The Source started to attract donations and received more than £5,000, so BCU had to apply to officially become a charity. This was eventually achieved in May 2017.

Questions for reflection

1. Have you ever talked to a homeless person, perhaps someone selling *The Big Issue*, or worked in a night shelter or a similar facility?

2. Cooking dinner in the night shelter was for me a big challenge. Have you ever experienced God's help as you stepped out in faith into a difficult role?

Eight
God's favour

Another opportunity: Easter 2015

We were given an opportunity to hold another witness stand, this time outside The Source. This took the form of an Easter Garden display. It was constructed from plywood and had a polystyrene base in which long plastic flower stems, each with a flower-head made of card, had been driven, thus creating the effect of a flower garden. This was set against a painted backdrop of an empty tomb, with a hill and crosses in the distance. People were given the opportunity to write a prayer request on a card flower shape and 'plant' it in the Easter garden. We gave out Easter eggs and also, in the second year, hot cross buns, which had been donated by the supermarket in the shopping centre.

This particular time of witness was not so easy to staff with volunteers, but in some way it had more impact and carried more importance, because, whereas nearly everybody knows about the Christian meaning of Christmas, this was not the case with the festival of Easter, particularly among those of other faiths. The 'prayer flowers' were very popular, and many good conversations with the public were possible: some people even made a commitment to God.

The Business Chaplaincy

By now (early 2015) we had an established permanent presence in the shopping centre. Simon Green had asked Mick if he could supply some kind of pastoral support to the shop workers in the complex. We called this the Vicarage Field Business Chaplaincy.

Mick was delighted to be given this opportunity and asked three or four church leaders if they would be willing to be involved. I knew nothing about this ministry, so in 2018 I interviewed Sylvia Weir of King's Church about her experience of leading it.

The Business Chaplaincy seems to be a quiet, rather obscure kind of ministry. It is very valuable but not attended by any kind of glamour or publicity. It needs no money, equipment or resources; just the time and commitment of the people involved. There are at present two chaplains, and Sylvia commits herself to visiting the shopping centre every week, seeing as many people as she can in the time. She prays for discernment before she goes to the centre, and that God will lead her to the people who are in need of encouragement. Sylvia says it is important to go weekly in order to establish relationships, especially as she is 'just popping in to say hello' a lot of the time.

Some businesses have a high turnover of staff. Sylvia is fortunate to be the kind of person who remembers names, and says she is always received very well, even by people of other faiths. They appreciate that someone is looking out for their welfare. Sometimes she hears personal stories, occasionally she is able to pray with someone, although this is rare owing to lack of privacy and time. Sometimes during Ramadan people are more open to conversations about God and faith, and some are surprised that Christians also fast. Sylvia points out that when we fast, we are able to hear God more clearly.

There is no drama in her ministry; just a consistent presence and a source of encouragement or comfort for someone who is perhaps bereaved or has a sick relative. It has been reported by a worker at the shopping centre that this chaplaincy has made a real difference to the people who work there, and they notice if Sylvia is away for any reason. At the time of writing, Sylvia has been a chaplain for three and a half years, since 2014. She may be the only Christian many people working in Vicarage Field will have meaningful contact with, and she believes in the 'priesthood of all believers'.[7] She also believes in the power of God working in the hearts of non-believers to draw them to Himself through these initial contacts. She really does represent 'Jesus in town'.

The Source

In The Source we have seen many people from the community helped in many ways. What a wonderful, God-sent opportunity this place provides, a focal point for the

---

[7] This is referred to in 1 Peter 2:9: 'You are a chosen people, a royal priesthood, a holy nation, God's special possession, that you may declare the praises of him who called you out of darkness into his wonderful light.'

work of God in the community. Working in the shop is not easy, and it is only for those who are skilled in dealing with the public. People come in for answers to queries about where to apply for housing because they have been evicted. They ask where they might be able to obtain free nappies or baby milk, or free food (we refer them to the Food Bank). Many people come for advice about benefits and are referred to the Job Centre. Some people come just for a chat or somewhere to rest for a while. Everyone is offered free tea or coffee and cakes, supplied by our food wholesale supplier, who donate 'use-by' dated food.

One of the principle tasks is to link night shelter users with our Night Shelter Operations Manager, who is given the task of finding accommodation for them so that we can have a steady turnover of guests from one year to the next. I was asked one day to take someone to see a flat which our contact had access to. I wrote about this in my diary, because the event made such an impression on me.

15th March 2015

Last week I was given the task of driving a night shelter guest to Erith in Kent to view a potential flat which he had been allocated. I dislike driving to strange places, particularly in the morning rush hour, but afterwards I was so glad to have done so. It made me realise afresh how blessed we are to have a good home to call our own. The place we saw was typical of a lot of rented accommodation now. A small three-bedroom house has been converted with a lock on every door to house as many people as possible; each room contains a bed, wardrobe, cooker and cupboard area which is converted to a tiny bathroom. There hardly seems to be room for the resident to turn around, let alone his possessions. But the place was clean and safe, and our night shelter friend was delighted, particularly as it was a short walk to the station for his morning commute. We as home owners take our homes for granted and do not really appreciate them.

Sometime the following summer I received a telephone call at home from Simon Green's secretary, wanting to arrange an urgent meeting with Mick. Many phone conversations ensued, back and forth. Mick worked, of course, in the school classroom all day and was therefore not free to make calls. We knew that this could be a very significant conversation; the question we were anticipating was, would Simon have to close us down or would he be able to help us further? We knew that things had not been easy in The Source lately and that the homeless folk had been there almost all the time. The ownership of the shopping centre had changed hands, another factor that made things a little uncertain.

Mick felt that God was in control and that He had everything in hand. When Mick went to see Simon, the new landlord's agent was present. When Mick arrived, the agent asked to him to share his story about The Source. This he did. Afterwards the agent said that he had heard the same story from others and that he was pleased with our work at Vicarage Field shopping centre. He then proposed a formal three-year tenancy agreement to run until October 2018, and added that he felt that our £1 rent per month was far too much. From now on it would be free. 'Let's do away with this peppercorn rent,' he said.

God had again provided us with an abundance of grace and favour, and we needed to take full advantage of being able to do the work He had for us in this wonderful opportunity.

Night shelter

Later in the year, in the winter season of the night shelter, we were contacted by a leader of a church in Thurrock who had heard of our work through a church member who owned a shop in Barking. They wanted to help, and at the same time to give their church members some experience of a night shelter ministry in operation.

One night a team of people from the church came to provide and cook a meal for the guests, and they also filled our car with donations of tinned food, as part of their Harvest giving. The place was full of helpers, all of whom enjoyed the evening and provided an extra source of interest for the guests, who had different people to talk to.

Connections with the BBC

In January 2016, Mick unexpectedly received a telephone call from someone from the BBC. A documentary was to be made about the cost of housing in London. The borough of Barking and Dagenham is known to have accommodation with the cheapest rent and the most affordable properties to buy, so the documentary was to include a visit to the borough. The local Council housing department was approached by the BBC and the staff there told them about our night shelter.

A night shelter committee meeting was held, to which representatives from the BBC were invited. We wanted to ensure that the night shelter would be portrayed in a positive light, and were assured that it would be. So, on several occasions from February through to May of that year a couple of young people visited the night shelter in the evenings to film the activity there and to interview various members of staff and guests. They specifically told the story of one of our guests, a professional lady from South Africa who had fallen on hard times.

The documentary was screened in October that year, entitled *No Place to Call Home*, and our ten-minute part of it was very insightful and complimentary about the work, setting the night shelter in the context of the wider housing shortage in London.

A visitor from Colombia

In 2016 we were given the opportunity to have a voluntary helper for a whole year, from a mission organisation called Time for God. Luis was twenty-two and had never been away from his home in Colombia, let alone in a foreign country with a completely different climate and way of life.

He arrived on a cold day in January, and he stayed in our house for the entire year. This proved to be something of a challenge at times, both for him and for me. He was very polite about my food, and about everything else that seemed strange to him, including the use of a duvet and the concept of winter clothes, of which he had brought none. Our first outing was to the shops to buy him something warm to wear.

Luis' mandate was to help in whatever way he could, so we mainly used him in The Source, which was now providing free lunches to the homeless. Luis is a fine Christian young man with a reasonable grasp of English. He was able to relate well to the men who frequented The Source daily, and was especially helpful if there were any Spanish speakers among them. He was able to pray with people and to tell them about his faith. When Luis left in December, he was greatly missed by us, whom he called his English father and mother, and especially by Amanda, The Source manager.

Questions for reflection

1. Have you seen evidence of God's favour being showered upon your church's outreach?

2. Could you start a business chaplaincy or set up an Easter outreach in your town?

Nine
Stories from The Source

The Source has become our primary centre in the marketplace and presence in the borough. The shopping centre management are very supportive and value our presence there. Many clients comment on the peaceful atmosphere and some on the sense of God's presence in The Source, and everyone finds a welcome and help of some kind.

It is a privilege that the churches have been given permission and permanent premises to establish God's work in the community in this way. The shop is committed to being open for most of the hours of the business day, to honour the gift of the use of the premises. The problem that The Source faces is a lack of willing helpers. It has two paid part-time managers, and everyone else comes as a volunteer. It is not a job for the faint-hearted; the person behind the desk needs to be ready to answer any query asked by the visitors and to be able to satisfy requests for advice, to signpost to other organisations, and to spot the need for prayer or a confidential chat and emotional support. If, as is the case for me, this is too daunting, there is always opportunity to serve food and clear up.

The Source's first part-time manager was Frances, who was sometimes joined by her husband, Steve, to give extra help on a Saturday. I interviewed them about some of their experiences.

One day, Frances told me, a Christian lady came in, saying that she didn't know quite why she was there but she had felt drawn towards The Source. She was closely followed by a Romanian lady, who did not speak English. The first lady was fluent in Romanian and was able to help Frances to identify the lady's needs.

For Steve, working in The Source in his free time gave him a break from his security work and a feeling of worth as he was able to help clients struggling with difficulties with landlords and unemployment, issues that he himself has had to deal with in the past. For Steve and Frances, working in The Source has given them an opportunity to 'give back' to the community and to God after they have been helped by others in the past. 'There but for the grace of God go I.'

Some people, Steve told me, don't seem to need much practical help. They just need a person to talk to, a friendly face, someone to understand. Steve and Frances have said that at times they felt like a father and mother to the clients. Both said that it was a very humbling experience, working to help very needy people, and has given them a new appreciation for their own, more stable and secure life.

One lady came in to The Source with a large deficit on her Oyster card,[8] more than £100. She did not know who to turn to. She had been summoned to a court in the centre of London and felt that this was very daunting and too far to go.

One of The Source staff was able to arrange for this lady to go to a local court instead, and contacted someone who was able to help her with her paperwork. One month later the lady had a job. The staff at The Source had given her the courage to face her problems and deal with them, she said.

In 2016 we were able to employ a second part-time manager, Amanda, and then later a third, Carol. Frances could then be released from the post, as she was finding the work more difficult now that the place was becoming so busy. She had been exactly the right person to begin the ministry, but now was the time for her to retire from this particular work.

---

[8] Oyster is a prepayment system to use the London Underground and London bus networks.

There is such a thing as a free lunch!

Tables were brought in to give the place more of the feel of a café. An allocated two-hour time-slot called Pit Stop was created, to provide lunch for the homeless. This lunch consists of a cold buffet of chicken pieces and pies, all of which can be heated in the microwave, as well as salad, fruit, bread, cheese and ham and usually plates of buns and cakes. I have made up salads from all kinds of combinations of vegetables, depending what is in the fridge on the day. I am always thankful that we can stop this perfectly good food from being wasted and meet the needs of the homeless people at the same time. A lot of the food comes from a large retailer some miles away in another commercial centre and has to be collected every week by a volunteer. It is food that is near its use-by date and the company gives it to charities. We also have local suppliers in Barking who donate chicken in the same way.

With the introduction of Pit Stop, the centre was able to host other initiatives at other times, such as a network for the bereaved, and a free English for Speakers of Other Languages (ESOL) class and a crafts therapy course of ten weeks called 'Peaced Together'. This therapeutic arts ministry enables a small group of people to come together to create beautiful objects to help them express and work through their emotional problems.

In July 2017 I interviewed Amanda about her experiences at The Source. I asked her to tell me about some of the challenges and the way God has answered prayers. She immediately spoke of the incredible, never-ending supply of food for the homeless. What we offer is in fact a kind of café service where everything is free, but this is only open to the homeless, who are vetted and verified to ensure that their needs are genuine before they become regular guests. The café is also open to those who are not homeless but can prove a genuine need.

'We have already fed more than 5,000,' Amanda said. 'Now I want to see the twelve baskets that were left over.' Not long before, God had told Amanda not to save food for the next day but to put everything out on the tables. Some of the volunteers at The Source did not like the way the guests filled their bags with food to take away for later, or even to share with friends. However, Amanda realised that this was the exact principle of the twelve baskets left over from the biblical account of the feeding of the 5,000 (Matthew 14:13-21).

It is a Christian principle that in order for God to bless us abundantly we have to first be prepared to give to others. This applies to our time as well as material resources. 'In order to see more of God's provision, we have to give it away,' said Amanda. So, they started to put all the day's excess food out on a table to be taken away in food bags. Suddenly they started to see an abundance – of chicken from two well-known chicken outlets, of pastries and bread from a high-street baker, and of money for food and toiletries from random donors.

'It's a banquet in comparison to what we did have.' Amanda said that she has sometimes put five plates of chicken out, knowing that it did not look like much for fifty people. Somehow the chicken has lasted for two entire sittings.

One day an Indian gentleman knocked at the door of The Source and offered two whole trolleys of bread, which comprised eighty loaves. A Muslim charity had received bread in answer to the Grenfell Tower disaster and had sent it to the Food Bank, who sent it to The Source.

Many people come through the door saying, 'I don't know why I am here; I just felt compelled to come.' Sometimes someone will pray for them, and they leave with renewed peace and confidence. 'What have you done?' they may say. 'I feel so much better.' Some people are encouraged to pray out loud for the first time, and to be open to the idea of a loving God who wants to help them.

An example of a practical problem Amanda had to deal with was a man who had not been able to pay his rent for six months because he had a problem with his pension.

Amanda was able to ring the Pensions office and get the money released and backdated. People have been sent to The Source from Citizens Advice, from the Job Centre and the local housing office. All these agencies know The Source as another source of help, literally.

Sometimes Amanda has had to call on God's protection in her role as manager. Once she was threatened by someone holding a knife and had to send for security. On another occasion a disturbed lady threw a hot cup of coffee straight at her, which nearly went all over Amanda. It covered the wall, which had to be repainted. Amanda prays before going to work, and she knows that God is surrounding her with a hedge of protection (see Job 1:10).

A constant challenge is the number of languages spoken by the clients. Somehow, however, there always seems to be someone around who can translate. Barriers have been broken down between people of different cultures, and the atmosphere in The Source is usually one of calm, and the peace and presence of God can be felt there. There is also a lot of banter and fun. At the end of a trying day Amanda has been known to let off steam by using the water gun hidden in her cupboard on an unsuspecting volunteer…

Help has come from unexpected places, as work at The Source has become more widely known. A local builder equipped the whole kitchen area with cupboards and new flooring, which he supplied himself, because he had once been homeless. A young man who also used to be homeless washes up the plates after Pit Stop. 'Because I have eaten here, I want to give back,' he says.

One day a lady came in to give a large bunch of flowers to Amanda, 'because I love you,' she said. 'Nobody else would help me.' Some of the men who come have really hard, tough exteriors, but their demeanours have been softened over the period of several weeks as they have attended The Source. They say Amanda is like a mother to them, and Jeanne and Nancy, two of our volunteers, are like their grandmas. People know that The Source is a place of safety where they will experience the love of God, even if they do not recognise it as such. With the combined services of Pit Stop and the rehousing officer employed by the night shelter, a lot of these men and women are integrated back into the community and able to access sustainable living. This is what the whole ministry is about: the restoration of broken lives wherever possible, and to give hope and encouragement.

On one of the days between Christmas 2017 and New Year 2018 Mick and I were working at The Source when a man came in who had been homeless for more than a year. He was partially deaf, and he wanted Mick to help him with a phone call to a housing agency who he hoped were about to offer him some accommodation. Mick duly made the call with him, and the man was offered an interview in a sheltered housing complex that same day. Although we were quite short-staffed, Mick drove him to the place and sat with him through the interview, which resulted in the man being offered a place that very day. He was absolutely delighted and so were we; what a lovely start to the New Year. He had no furniture, so Mick emailed all the churches, and furniture was donated within the week.

In my time volunteering at The Source I have observed human nature at its most desperate. The men who come to Pit Stop are usually there because they are hungry, and the meal we give them might be the only proper meal they will have that day. Sometimes we see bad manners, and at other times we see gentleman-like politeness. We have to be wary about how much food we put out at a thirty-minute lunch session, to be sure that the food will last for the full two hours we are open. Perhaps twenty men might come to the door all at once at 12.00, and then another thirty people will arrive after 12.30. After Christmas 2017 we started to see around seventy people a day at Pit Stop. Some are respectful of the needs of others; some try to quietly shovel pieces of chicken into their bags. It is at first easy to be judgemental of such behaviour, but then we have to realise that if we were in their place we might react the same way, but for the grace of God in our lives. Although there is always enough food, its distribution has to be managed sensibly because people sometimes want to take too much. We make sure that everyone is fed a good meal, and there are usually extra cakes and snacks to take away.

Questions for reflection

1. Amanda stepped out in faith to give away surplus food. Could your ministry do the same, perhaps to help somebody else's ministry?

2. Would you consider sharing resources, staff time, lending equipment or material goods to help a ministry run by another church?

Ten
Companions

I do not know when I first became aware of the needs of the housebound elderly in our local community. Perhaps I had always been interested in them – maybe this stemmed from my work in two nursing homes when I was younger. In December 2010 I volunteered to drive two elderly residents of the borough to a Christmas party run by the volunteer bureau. At the party I was talking to some of the guests, and at least one lady said that she did not know her neighbours and had no friends in the area. When I took the ladies home, I asked one of them if she would like to receive a regular visit from someone. 'Oh, yes please,' was her reply. 'I get so lonely.'

As Christians we are commanded to serve each other and to 'do good to all people' (Galatians 6:10). We should, as church members, naturally keep an eye on the vulnerable people in our churches, offer to help people with housework if they are sick, provide transport to hospital, and so on. These are small services which should be performing for each other, and some of the elderly people in our churches have no one else. When we lived in Manor Park, we as a family had close relationships with several elderly ladies over the years, and one became an honorary granny to our children.

Unfortunately, this kind of care does not always take place in church family life, perhaps because of our busy lifestyles which prohibit us from committing time to people outside our own immediate family members, and perhaps a lack of openness with each other about our needs. The mask of pride says, 'Yes, my husband is sick but we don't need any help.' We don't want people to think that we can't cope, and we do not want to feel obligated to anyone.

But how many times have I been on the receiving end of the generosity and kindness of other church members? House-cleaning when I was ill, babysitting regularly when our children were small so my husband and I could relax together, help with sewing projects, window cleaning... the list goes on, and I will be forever grateful to my Lord God who sent each person to me.

As we minister to each other in these ways, how good it is to extend this help to others outside our own church, both in other churches and in our local community. Many Christians commute to a church outside their local neighbourhood and, as we get to know people in our local communities, we can sometimes offer support where their own church members are too far away to offer regular practical support.

I include an excerpt from my diary in 2012:

I have been trying to establish a service called 'Companions' for volunteers to visit elderly people once a week, drawing on members of our local churches. I have been visiting Hazel ... for two years now. She does see her daughters at weekends but between them she is alone all day except for the agency carers who get her dressed and put her to bed. I enjoy our weekly visits; Hazel has a good sense of humour and we are enjoying a biography together. Hazel is partially sighted and cannot read, so I am reading the book to her. I chose the autobiography of M M Kaye, author of The Far Pavilions, *in which she describes her life growing up in India in the 1920s. Hazel really identifies with the book; she knew many of the scenes described by the author.*

'You are talking about my memories. It is such a joy,' she would say. Then we would read a bit more, and stop and agree or disagree with Mollie Kaye's pithy observations on human nature.

Because Hazel does not go out except with her daughter at weekends, I tell her the small goings on of my week; some weeks are more interesting than others. She really values the time I spend and, although I am sometimes busy, I am always glad that I went.

I have been trying to recruit a workforce for this ministry as I know there must be many residents in the community who need a visitor, but have so far been unsuccessful. It seemed such a simple thing to do, but many people are wary of getting involved in a long-term commitment of this nature. Also, many people have to visit their own elderly parents.

This regular commitment to Hazel was sometimes a bit of a challenge; not because I did not enjoy my visits, but because I sometimes thought I should be doing my own chores or running errands in the time I had set aside in my head. From the beginning I always stayed at least an hour, and usually an extra half hour, because I imagined how I might feel if I was lonely all day and someone came to see me and left after twenty minutes. This is why it was really useful to share a book together. I remember reading in the novels of Jane Austen how ladies who went 'calling' in the afternoon would stay for a socially acceptable fifteen minutes, talking of fashions and gossiping about acquaintances, before moving on to the next visit! How much better to really share life's ups and downs and to get to know someone properly, allowing them to reminisce and tell stories, comment on the latest news and perhaps pray together for a few minutes. I continued visiting Hazel for nearly five years until her death, and I valued our time together as a little oasis of calm in a busy week.

To this date I have not been successful in beginning a volunteering and visiting ministry, but I am hopeful that one day something can be done with the resources of people we have in the churches.

Questions for reflection

1. Are you aware of any elderly and lonely people near to you?

2. Have you ever volunteered at the local elderly lunch club?

Part Two

The Challenge

In this part of the book we will be discussing the practicalities we had to consider in establishing some of our ministries. We will also look at the scriptural applications and spiritual issues, and include some biblical teaching relevant to the ministries we believe we have been led by God to establish.

Eleven
A strong prayer foundation – and a vision

Guidance and timing

The primary preparation needed before any new ministry of evangelism or community work can begin is a period of time praying about the plans, asking God to supply the ideas, or the people, or the place in which to begin, or sometimes all three. This period of time may continue for several weeks, months or even years. We always have to wait for God's perfect timing, and He has a way of making the time known to us, by perhaps a phone call from someone unconnected with our plans, or a chance meeting, or a set of circumstances that naturally lead into a series of things coming together at a specific time. We do know that if we experience a desire to start a ministry it is usually one that God has placed in our hearts, and therefore we are praying in accordance with His will.

Jesus said in the Gospel of John, 15:16, 'I chose you and appointed you so that you might go and bear fruit – fruit that will last – and so that whatever you ask in my name the Father will give you.'

Praying with a friend, or maybe two, is sometimes a very good way of experiencing God's guidance, because then the friend may confirm what we think God is saying. It may be that a friend has a gift of prophecy or can 'see' pictures with their spiritual eyes, which will confirm what we think God is saying. The BIN has often been a setting for receiving prophetic words. A word from a stranger may also be used by God, or a completely unconnected and unexpected message, like a billboard or a poster on a bus. The different ways in which God speaks to people are endless and varied, and very personal. The key requirement is to be open to impressions and ideas from God and to be obedient to His call.

Examples of these impressions received from God are here explored. Mick takes over the account at this point to explain in his own words the pictures and their meanings.

Many words and pictures have been given to me about how the church can transform communities for Jesus. I believe that there are three significant pictures that are of key importance in taking our town for Jesus. The first picture or word of knowledge is that of a fishing net full of fish, the second is that of a poster saying, 'Think Big', and the third is that of an umbrella. The exposition of these pictures and words from God are explained below.

1. Fishing net picture

This is a picture I received from someone with a prophetic gift in Barking in 2010, who saw that God would use me to facilitate a transformation in the town. He saw that Barking would be like a fisherman's net and that I would facilitate a move of the churches to work together in prayer and community ministries to draw people to come to Jesus. A great number of fishes would be gathered in this net, and all that would be required would be to take the fish out of the net and take them home for consumption.

The interpretation of this picture is that a large number of people who don't know Jesus would come into these ministries (such as The Source), and the role of the church would be to collect them, take them to their church, bring them to Christ and disciple them. In Barking town centre there is a monument with a similar picture, which reminds me of this word from God.

This fishing net picture prophecy has been fulfilled, as by the end of 2018 we were having around 1,100 people who do not know Jesus visit The Source every month. These people are symbolically in the fishing net. Jesus said

His disciples were to be 'fishers of men' (Mark 1:17, ESV UK).

I visited a church in Broadstairs in 2017, and above the altar another picture which included a fishing net was displayed.[9]

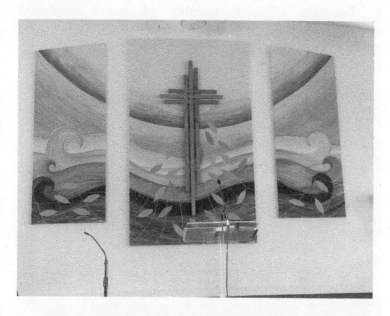

I believe that God is saying that when the church comes together with a kingdom attitude and mindset in prayer and united community ministry, God will draw the people of the town into a large net that is bursting at its seams, and when this happens, all the churches will need to do is to take the fish (people) out of the net and disciple them in their churches. The challenge is for the churches to rise to this challenge and send workers into the place of the net.

---

[9] Queens Road Baptist Church, Broadstairs. Image used with permission.

We need a 'Go to them' strategy rather than saying 'Come to us'.

2. 'Think Big' picture

In February 2016, a number of buses displayed advertisements for a large second-hand car outlet. The adverts said, 'Think Bigger'.

At the same time, a man from outside Barking, who had a gift of prophecy and had little knowledge of me, approached me and said that God was telling me to extend my tent posts and to 'Think Big'.

> Enlarge the place of your tent,
> stretch your tent curtains wide,
> do not hold back;

lengthen your cords,
strengthen your stakes.
For you will spread out to right and to the
left …
Do not be afraid.
Isaiah 54:2-4

(From here Elizabeth resumes the narrative.)

Both these words came to Mick in the same week, and he knew they were linked to each other, so he waited for God to provide a full explanation of what they meant.

A month later he went to Chicago, USA, for work purposes and had the opportunity to visit Willow Creek Church. There he saw how the church on a large scale was engaging and meeting the needs of the community for free, demonstrating God's love and compassion. God also impressed on him the need to change his mindset and attitude, to think big and to raise his expectations of what He could do in Barking if we would look to the Him to be the God of the 'Himpossible'.

As if this was not enough to confirm what God was saying to Mick, the following month we went on holiday to Ibiza. While we were on a local bus visiting the local sights, the bus stopped. When we looked across the road, we saw a large billboard poster on which were the words, 'Think Big'.

'The Spirit of the Lord is on me,
because he has anointed me
to proclaim good news to the poor.
He has sent me to proclaim freedom for the
prisoners

and recovery of sight for the blind,
to set the oppressed free,
to proclaim the year of the Lord's favour.'
Luke 4:18-19

The Lord would say:

'Come, you who are blessed by my Father; take
your inheritance, the kingdom prepared for
you since the creation of the world. For I was
hungry and you gave me something to eat, I
was thirsty and you gave me something to
drink, I was a stranger and you invited me in, I
needed clothes and you clothed me, I was ill
and you looked after me.'
Matthew 25:34-36

Over the following months God continued to speak to Mick about this and encouraged him to dream bigger for ministries in Barking and The Source and to increase his efforts to bring churches together in prayer and community ministry and to usher the presence of God into the town.

Mick writes:

> The Lord is saying we all need to think 'Big' because together He has made us 'Big'. But we have made ourselves 'Smaller' because we operate mainly on our own. However, in our oneness He has made us 'Big'. Together we need to step out in faith rather than fear to see God become bigger in Barking and in Barking Churches Unite.
>
> The local church needs to have a Big vision and see the 'Big' picture. Luke 4:18 is a mandate and manifesto to the church. The big vision is for the town to know Jesus and the big picture is for God's presence and kingdom to take over the town. For this to be realised, the church needs to embrace both Luke 4:18 and the second commandment, which is to love our neighbour as ourselves, and in this we will become united in mission and will work as a united team to reach out to all inhabitants, rich and poor, and proclaim the gospel.
>
> We need to bring healing by meeting the needs of our neighbours and making relationships, in so doing bring deliverance, peace, joy and salvation.

The church needs to pray the prayer of Jabez: 'Oh, that you would bless me and enlarge my territory! Let your hand be with me, and keep me from harm' (1 Chronicles 4:10).

The Lord continued to speak to Mick through the prayer of Jabez, as well as through Isaiah 54:2-3 and Jeremiah 29:11: '"For I know the plans I have for you," declares the Lord, "plans to prosper you and not to harm you, plans to give you hope and a future."' Out of these pictures and scriptures has come the Christian Community Care Centre picture and vision – a plan Mick believes God has given him for future ministry in Barking. He writes:

Some people say, 'I serve God in my own little way.'

Why don't we start serving God in a bigger way? Why not let Him use us more?

'Well, I'm fine the way I am. That's the way God made me,' they say.

God has made us to be 'Big', not 'Small'. We confuse small thinking with spirituality. God has empowered His church to think big and not small for Him. We need to believe in the God of the 'Himpossible'. God has provided us and His church with all the tools we need to transform communities. The bottom line is this: if we think and dream 'Big', we get into the mindset of seeking God and hearing His voice, and asking God to enlarge the territory of His kingdom to encompass our whole town.

We need to consider the mandate of the Great Commission in the strategy of our life and church in this 'Big' thinking. How much time do we as a church work in our community? How much time do we spend serving God in our community reaching out to the hungry and those who do not know God? God has shown us reckless love so that we can show reckless love to our community. In the parable of the lost sheep, the shepherd leaves the ninety-nine sheep, which are safe already in the pen, to find the one that is lost and bring it back to safety (Luke 15:3-7). That is our mission: to 'Go' and find the lost and to understand that a 'Come' strategy is not what God has commanded. Through our 'Going', people 'Come' to know God.

How much time does the church spend going into the local community? How much time does your church spend engaging in meeting the community's needs? How much time did Jesus spend in the community meeting needs? The answer to this third question is most of the time. That is the example that God was showing us. If we are to extend our territory and take our town for Jesus, we need to come out from within our four walls and spread across our town, so that the town will know God's love and compassion and so that the town will be known as God's town and territory.

Wherever we go, we carry God's power and authority. Wherever we go, we carry His presence and the Holy Spirit. Wherever we go, we can carry God's deliverance to the people. Wherever we go, we can bring God's healing, redemption and salvation. Wherever we go, we can transform our town. We just need to reverse our mindset from 'Small' to 'Big'.

In some places, the united church is taking responsibility for voluntary services without conditions. This is the 'Big' picture. This is the vision of the Christian Community Care Centre: to be the church working in our town, praying for people, making relationships, meeting needs and then bringing people to know God.

Some might say, 'We can't bring our town to know God. It's too big. We don't have the resources. We are ants in this town and cannot affect what goes on. We can only do a little bit.'

Even if we do not say this outright, our actions and strategies often seem to reflect it. When we move to a 'Big' mindset we move from I CAN'T to I CAN. We are more than conquerors through Christ Jesus. We serve the God of the impossible. So therefore, if we stand together, we can take our town for Jesus. Can't we?

Expect great things from God and attempt great things for God. If we have faith, God will give us the necessary power. He loves to use ordinary people who are willing to trust Him, and to see them succeed. All the major characters in the Bible were not 'Big' for God, but through their simple faith and trust in God they became 'Big'. Moses, Abraham, Peter and Paul all felt 'Small' in what they could do, but in God they became 'Big'.

God spoke further to Mick as he continued to seek Him, to show him more of this 'Big' vision, and towards the end of the year the Lord showed him a third picture, that of an umbrella. From vision comes strategy; from these will come fruit. The umbrella depicts a strategy.

3. U for unity; U for umbrella

It is often when churches are seeking the will of God together that He makes things happen. Mick received from the Lord a vision of an umbrella which he feels depicts the idea of different churches coming to work together in the community.

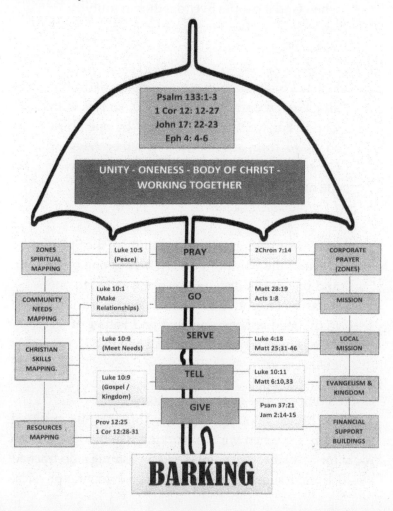

The canopy of the umbrella represents the united church. This unity reflects the Father's heart for His people to demonstrate His love and compassion in their community, and to be His witnesses, reflecting His presence and love to needy people.

> How good and pleasant it is
> when God's people live together in unity …
> For there the Lord bestows his blessing.
> *Psalm 133:1, 3*

> Just as a body, though one, has many parts, but all its many parts form one body, so it is with Christ. For we were all baptised by one Spirit so as to form one body – whether Jews or Gentiles, slave or free – and we were all given the one Spirit to drink.
> *1 Corinthians 12:12-13*

> Make every effort to keep the unity of the Spirit through the bond of peace. There is one body and one Spirit, just are you were called to one hope when you were called; one Lord, one faith, one baptism; one God and Father of all, who is over all and through all and in all.
> *Ephesians 4:3-6*

Church unity brings about six outcomes:
1. Unity brings about protection. This may be spiritual protection, for when we are working together there is no room for petty disagreements or for becoming side-tracked by doctrinal issues. There may even be evident a physical

protection when churches are united in purpose; for example, if a Council or local government were to have any concerns about the work of a church, perhaps leaders from another church may be able to write letters or to petition authorities on their behalf.

2. Unity expresses our love in diversity.

3. Unity brings about God's blessing and power.

4. Unity breaks strongholds. This is a spiritual concept, meaning that the power of standing together in prayer can have consequences in heaven that bring about a change of circumstances here on earth.

5. Unity brings the family of God together.

6. Unity brings about transformation – we get things done by working together.

Unity gives a foretaste of heaven itself, where we will all truly be one.

The spine of the umbrella represents how we can bring the kingdom of God into the town and engages the Commissioning Principle in Luke 10:2-10:

> 'The harvest is plentiful, but the workers are few ... Go! I am sending you out like lambs among wolves ...
> 'When you enter a house, first say, "Peace to this house." [Pray.] ...
> 'Stay there, eating and drinking whatever they give you. [Make relationships.] ...
> 'Heal those who are ill. [Meet needs.] ...
> 'Tell them, "The kingdom of God has come near to you." [Tell them about the gospel and

be prepared to back up your witness with an authentically Christian lifestyle.]

1. Pray (Luke 10:5)
Pray individually. Pray peace and blessings over people wherever you go. Pray over letters you send out. Pray when you pass a home or enter the office. Pray over phone calls. Pray that God will provide opportunities to get to know your neighbours. Pray corporately as one church through corporate zone prayer gatherings as adults, children and youth, in street praying, intercessory prayer groups, and as leaders coming together to pray for one another and for your ministries.

> If my people, who are called by my name, will humble themselves and pray and seek my face and turn from their wicked ways, then will I hear from heaven and will forgive their sin and will heal their land.
> *2 Chron 7:14*

2. Go (Luke 10:1)
The church is unique in that it exists for the benefit of those outside its membership. We should always be mission-focused rather than inward-looking, thinking of 'them', not 'us'; 'you', not 'me'.

Our strategy, as mentioned before, should be to 'Go' rather than to say 'Come'. Like Jesus, we are to seek the lost sheep. The call to 'Go' is simply to make relationships and friendships with people in the world. Individually we are called to be God's witnesses wherever we go and to be salt and light in all aspects of the marketplace including government, education, business, media, leisure, family life and among those of other faiths. This call to 'Go' also involves local missions, ministries to the poor (such as soup kitchens, night shelters, food banks), business chaplaincy and education prayer networks. Pray for opportunities to enjoy fellowship and make relationships.

> Devote yourselves to prayer, being watchful and thankful. And pray for us, too, that God may open a door for our message, so that we may proclaim the mystery of Christ.
> *Colossians 4:2-3*

Wherever you 'Go', you carry the kingdom and Spirit of God and His presence within you. Your intimacy and relationship with God will affect your workplace, street and church.

3. Serve (Luke 10:9)
Serving is about meeting the needs of people in whatever way we can, from our resources, both practical and spiritual (ie praying for them).

The Lord would say:

> 'Come, you who are blessed by my Father; take your inheritance, the kingdom prepared for you since the creation of the world. For I was hungry and you gave me something to eat, I was thirsty and you gave me something to drink, I was a stranger and you invited me in, I needed clothes and you clothed me, I was ill and you looked after me.'
> *Matthew 25:34-36*

We can do this individually by serving in local community ministries such as night shelters, local Christian facilities in the town such as The Source, running or volunteering in a chaplaincy to serve a business or a hospital, or by operating or volunteering at a children's club or after-school facility. We can work corporately as churches by supporting and getting behind the local ministries, meeting their needs and serving the community and the poor.

4. Tell (Luke 10:9)

Telling people about Jesus comes naturally when you have a relationship with them and you have unconditionally met their needs. Telling people how God impacts and works in your life should not be difficult. We are all called to be His witnesses, not just those who are called to be evangelists or paid clergy. I need to be prepared to share in a few minutes what my friend Jesus has done for me, what I was before I met Him and what my life with Jesus is like now, and to tell others that they can have the same experience and intimacy with Him and God as Father too. Witnesses tell their version of an event, their own story.

5. Give

A generous person will prosper;
whoever refreshes others will be refreshed.
Proverbs 11:25

The righteous give generously.
Psalm 37:21

> For just as each of us has one body with many members, and these members do not all have the same function, so in Christ we, though many, form one body, and each member belongs to all the others.
> *Romans 12:4-5*

This aspect of the umbrella affects individuals and churches giving to the united purpose of community faith action. Individuals give by using their spiritual and practical gifts, their time and their finances. Churches can give by using their buildings and by being willing to share their resources, time and finances for local mission. If churches work together and each one owns a share in the mission, it will have a bigger impact on those who see it, and show them the effectiveness of our unity.

Under the canopy of the umbrella

The relevance of the area under the umbrella is that the united church acts as a protection to those under it, namely the town. In order to provide protection, the united church needs to map its area in four ways and then needs to collate the information.

1. Spiritual zone mapping
Spiritual mapping involves physically dividing the town, borough or county into zones on a map. We did this through street praying walks and praying over a map of Barking. We discovered that our findings coincided with the way the Council had separated the area into wards.

The next thing is to find out what the spiritually negative aspects of each street and zone are (for example, depression, oppression, anger, pride, self-reliance). We did this through opening ourselves to God and asking Him to show us in a word that relates to the overriding spiritual problem of the place. The revelation of this may occur in a quiet prayer time or in a corporate prayer time where someone is given a strong impression of something from the Lord. It may be a revelation received on a prayer walk. Some of our intercessors have the spiritual gift of discernment and prophecy, and they are often used by God to confirm or to bring new words.

The location of the churches in each zone is plotted on the map (see chapter one for prayer zone map).

Street praying is the main key to being able to plot these things and to being able to discern the community needs.

2. Community needs mapping

It is vitally important that the united church identifies the practical needs of each zone and street in order to facilitate mission and meet the zone's needs (such as poverty, debt, elderly residents living alone, domestic violence, youth crime, unemployment, homelessness, prostitution, drugs). It is a waste of time and resources to provide something that is not required. Mission is then planned around these identified areas. Community needs are discovered through surveys, Council research and statistics, and the local newspaper. We have found that each zone has its own individual characteristic needs and environment.

3. Christian skills mapping

For the united church to meet the needs of the local community, each individual church needs to find out the skills and spiritual giftings of its workforce and its members and collectively use these giftings to further the unity and transformation of a town. (The Being kingdom people resource sheet and Talents profile in Appendices 4 and 3 are helpful for this task.)

4. Resources mapping

This last aspect relates to mapping the resources of each church and offering these for the purpose of building God's kingdom in the town. These resources may take the form of money, premises, equipment, and so on. A survey across the churches could accomplish this aim. (See the Being a kingdom church resource sheet in Appendix 5.)

The umbrella handle

The function of the handle of the umbrella is that it enables the person to hold it. Without the handle, the umbrella would blow away. Our handle is God and having a kingdom attitude and mindset to bring about the transformation of our community. We need to symbolically bring God's presence and invite the Holy Spirit to work in the hearts of people in the town. We need to have a passion to tell people in our town about Christ. We must be willing to receive and disciple these people in our churches. We need a large, structured and purposeful vision.

Questions for reflection

1. Have you a vision for a particular ministry? Have you a prayer partner or a small group to pray with until it comes to fruition?

2. Are you aware of people in other churches who share the same vision?

3. Do you have opportunities to support someone in need of prayer?

4. Has any form of spiritual mapping taken place in your town? Could this be achieved?

5. Are churches willing to join together to do this, and to pool their resources?

6. How will you devise a strategy?

Twelve
Communication

It is vital to keep good communication links alive, especially when working with a number of churches. This is where holding regular meetings for the church leaders has been useful, to keep them updated on the progress of the various ministries. Many of them have been too busy with their own church business to keep abreast of what is happening, so a regular breakfast together five times a year has helped. These breakfasts have also offered opportunities to pray together and to share ideas and problems as leaders, and to deepen friendships.

Events should be planned and published at the beginning of a year where possible, to enable church leaders to include them in their own church calendars.

The ambassador

Appointing an 'ambassador' for BCU in as many churches as possible has been valuable. These ambassadors are invariably people who attend the united prayer meetings, at which the most up-to-date news is presented, and they are integrally involved in at least one BCU ministry or prayer group. They can then communicate enthusiasm and a personal interest back in their church, and encourage others to get involved. They can also promote events or announce ministry opportunities to keep church members informed.

Prayer meetings

The united prayer meetings which happen five times a year are not only times of prayer for the work, but also opportunities to share news and specific needs, be they financial or for more helpers, or for prayer for God to move in a particular way. These meetings are valuable communication opportunities, from which those attending can receive a true picture of the ministry and can communicate to their wider networks. Part of the meeting usually focuses on one particular ministry and prayer for the leader, and they will be given some time to speak. We often make a collection for this ministry in the meeting, too.

The BCU coordinator

The overall coordinator of a potentially large and complex organisation like BCU needs to be someone with a vision and a passion, and who can discern the will of God. They should have a calling from God and should see this role as their primary ministry. They must also be recognised and acknowledged by the church leaders as the right person to head up the work. However, they should not be a church leader. This is because a church leader must be primarily concerned with the needs of their church and prioritise these over everything else. When dates of events clash, for example, they would be expected to attend the event at their own church, and to encourage others in the congregation to do the same.

A united churches and missions coordinator in a town needs to be free to attend any church in the town, without being considered disloyal. There may be times when they will not attend their own church for several weeks at a time, as they will be visiting other churches to network with the leaders.

It is important that the coordinator is able to relate to people and make friendships, however superficial, with leaders of lots of different denominations, in order to be able to keep everyone interested in the work. Mick is particularly good at this, being a gregarious character who is well respected and liked. But it has taken him time and effort to achieve this status, and he often has to go out to meet people and attend all sorts of church functions.

The apostle Paul says:

> Though I am free and belong to no one, I have made myself a slave to everyone, to win as many as possible. To the Jews I became like a Jew, to win the Jews. To those under the law I became like one under the law (though I myself am not under the law), so as to win those under the law ... I have become all things to all people so that by all possible means I might save some.
> *1 Corinthians 9:19-20, 22*

Mick has developed a very sympathetic and embracing viewpoint towards all types of denominations, which has expanded his outlook.

One of the most important things Mick tries to do is to visit every church in the town at least once a year and, if possible, to talk with the church leader. When he visits a church, he can often deduce its strengths, identify its main ministries and meet those in the congregation who have certain visions or passions for different ministries. Sometimes he obtains their permission to pass on their details to similarly minded people in other churches.

Social media

The use of Facebook, WhatsApp, emails and websites are important communication tools to publicise events and to provide a forum to share ideas. Mick sends details of meetings and events to all the leaders through Facebook. WhatsApp is a great tool for finding resources and communicating quickly. For example, we collected furniture for a man in need by contacting everyone in the group to find out whether they knew of anything that was available.

Written aids

Leaflets for the congregation members have been useful to advertise and remind people of events, street praying or other meetings. These are usually delivered to the churches to be distributed the Sunday morning before an event.

Prayer diary

Again, this can be a useful tool to remind people of upcoming events and can be used as an aid to prayer for all types of subjects and needs in the borough as well as in the churches. It can also identify ministries to the congregations of different churches, so that the members can perhaps engage in these ministries.

Questions for reflection

1. How does communication work in your ministry?

2. Is it effective?

3. Do you have a coordinator for church unity? Are they also a church leader?

Thirteen
Ministry and mission

Establishing a night shelter ministry

The establishment of and running of a night shelter has proven to be a very challenging and demanding task, not one to be taken on lightly. There are a great many legal obligations and procedures to be dealt with: the local Council has to be approached, money has to be raised constantly, and there are safety and vetting procedures for guests and helpers.

Many things need to be considered when contemplating a venture of this kind, especially if the shelter has to move between locations, as is the case for us. Had we a venue for seven nights we would not have had to find, maintain and use a trailer every night. This trailer contains all of the night shelter equipment: cooking pots and utensils, all the bedding and towels for the guests, boxes of toiletries and, of course, the staple food items for our mobile store cupboard: cooking oil, salt, sugar, coffee, breakfast supplies, the urn and mugs... the list goes on. One advantage of having to store everything in the trailer, however, is that we know it will be available for the following day, unless anything has been left behind or broken in transit. This rarely happens, fortunately.

Otherwise we are reliant on using whatever cooking equipment we find in the different church kitchens.

There are a lot of legal requirements that have to be dealt with before a ministry of this kind can be started. Premises have to be found which are easy for all the homeless people to access. If it is not possible for the night shelter to be based in one place, several premises must be found. There must be enough decent-sized rooms: one for the men to sleep in, another for the women, a kitchen that is properly equipped to cook a meal for twenty or so people, at least two toilets and washing facilities, and a secure door. Ideally the premises should have a couple of showers. The premises must have the required fire extinguishers and fire safety doors and the kitchen must satisfy the legal hygiene and cleanliness requirements. (Of course, these standards should automatically be met in a church building anyway.)

Some board games, a pool table or table tennis facilities all add an extra dimension to the evening. Obviously, these additions are dependent on the amount of space in the venue.

Beds must be provided, and if they have to be collapsed and moved every night, they must be sturdy. Mattresses must be clean and as portable as possible. In our case they have to be loaded into a van every night, which adds to the wear and tear. Bedding must be washed regularly.

Food must be of the best quality possible. Night shelter guests deserve good, nourishing, hot meals, especially as the meal they get here may well have to last them until the next evening. The food has to be sourced – a consistent supply to feed thirty people night after night with no money involved. Transport and collection of this food has to be arranged, as well as the correct storage.

The people working as volunteers for this work must not be easily offended by bad language or rudeness, and they need to be sensitive to the mood of the guests, and able to banter and be relaxed with them. It is no good being a 'super-holy' type of person who cannot make allowances for others. I remember my mother as a woman who exuded the love of Jesus wherever she could. She volunteered for some years in a soup kitchen in Worcester, and she found the attitudes of some of the guests hard to cope with, but she did it with a good grace and accepting them and their problems. (For years she regularly bought *The Big Issue* to help her local homeless people, a long time before I was involved in a night shelter.)

Most importantly, the volunteers have to be completely committed to serving in the night shelter, as there will be no one to replace them if they cannot be there. Most of our volunteers come on a monthly or a fortnightly basis, and all are completely faithful and dependable. They are very much aware of the vital importance of this kind of work, and all derive great satisfaction from it.

Several teams of people are needed for different times of the operation. First, there must be a small group of people to cook dinner, to be able to arrive early enough to provide a hot meal an hour or so after the night shelter opens its doors. Many guests do not want to be waiting a long time for dinner. They are hungry, and they are also usually very tired and want to go to bed soon afterwards.

Ideally, another team of people is needed to spend time with the guests, especially if the whole focus of the ministry is to tell them about the gospel. It is very helpful if these people are able to go regularly, to befriend the guests and to get to know them, perhaps even to pray with them as time goes by.

A paid manager has been an important person in our night shelter. He can deal with any rowdiness and can sleep there overnight, to guarantee security of the guests.

A third small team of people, or perhaps one individual, is needed to come in the morning to prepare a simple breakfast, if this is being provided, and to clean and lock up the venue when all the guests have left.

Safeguarding training should be put in place for the volunteers. Sensible rules must be observed at all times; the personal safety of both volunteers and guests is paramount, and chaperoning rules should be in place and personal details kept confidential.

Rules are (sometimes) made to be broken

A venture of this kind has to have strict rules and structures. However, a certain amount of discernment is needed for particular situations. For example, we have a general rule that no one is allowed in if they have been drinking. We have had to call the police or threaten to call the police on many occasions when certain individuals have arrived very late and drunk and caused a disturbance. However, there have been at least two occasions when an inebriated guest has arrived and stayed a little while for a chat or had dinner or just dozed in a chair for a while. Before evicting them immediately, a chat is helpful.

A guest arrived one evening and had clearly been drinking. The team leader, Natasha, wisely invited him for a private chat before excluding him. After a little while he started to foam at the mouth. Natasha knew this meant he had combined his alcohol with drugs. She called an ambulance immediately when he showed more signs of crisis, and they dealt with him and saved his life. Natasha stayed with the man, accompanied him to hospital and acted as his next of kin. If we had evicted him for drunkenness, he would have surely died that night on the streets.

Another occasion we had some problems was in May of the second season, the last night of the shelter for the season. We had provided a barbecue and had a birthday cake for a guest. Quite a few of the men were very unsettled because they knew they would be sleeping rough again the next night. An intoxicated guest arrived. He had just heard that his mother was dying of cancer – she actually only survived for another week, we later found out. We let him stay because he was quiet and not being disruptive.

That evening we also had a special guest speaker, Terry, who had come to give his testimony about his deliverance by God from homelessness and crime. As soon as he started to speak, the 'birthday' guest started to heckle him, contradicting and interrupting Terry because he took offence at the message. So he was ushered outside. Once outside he was comforted by Mick and broke down on hearing about God's love.

As soon as Terry left, the guests calmed down and a peaceful night followed; the only sounds were snores. Two or three of the volunteers were able to talk to the 'birthday guest' and to the inebriated man. If we had evicted the men, we would not have been able to demonstrate God's love to them and they would have felt rejected on the last night of the shelter, ending the season on an unhappy note.

The next morning everything went smoothly; all the men cheerfully loaded the mattresses onto the trailer and said goodbye.

There is a happy follow-up story regarding one of the men. Six months on, he rededicated his life to God, has stopped drinking and is now working in a night shelter in Havering, ministering to homeless men.

When the guests are able to confide the details of their stories, we realise how hard their lives have been, and still are, and we have to remember that they are truly desperate to humble themselves to come to us. Also, most of them have no personal faith in God to give them hope or motivation, and they are often far away from family or friends. Some of them band together over the six months and form friendships within the group.

Logistics

The trailer which contains all the beds and the tea urn and other vital equipment has to be taken to each venue. This is the most challenging of the tasks to be performed, because the whole operation depends on its prompt arrival every night. Many have been the weekend visits to a company to buy yet another 'jockey wheel', a mysteriously named and apparently not very robust yet essential part of the trailer equipment. The three men who move the trailer have to maintain their own cars with the requisite tow bars, and they are dependent on each other for cover if one is sick or on holiday. Many times, Mick has had to help, and for the first four years he was part of the trailer team.

Over the years there have been some surprise dilemmas, some of which have been very interesting. Once I came home from work to find that my small porch was completely full of bin bags of clothes, which a well-meaning person had placed there, obviously as donations for the night shelter. I had to force my way past them into the house. I had no room in my lounge for all the bags, so the only alternative was to offload them somewhere as soon as possible. On closer inspection, a lot of the bags contained extremely unsuitable high-heeled shoes, children's clothes and evening dresses! I was not pleased. To make matters worse, I had no car at the time, and Mick was in Romania for the week. So I had to lug the bags on a train, bit by bit, to Barking and East Ham on my way to work, to charity shops, keeping just a small bag of the donated clothes for the night shelter guests.

Another time, in November 2015, Mick received a phone call at about 10 pm from Steve Hanna, the vicar of St Elisabeth's Church and one of the night shelter trustees. 'There's a man with a refrigerated van of frozen chicken pieces in my driveway. He has brought them here instead of throwing them away. What am I going to do with them all?'

Now, that's not the kind of question Steve was expecting to have to ask at that time of night! About an hour and a lot of phone calls later we had been able to arrange for most of the chicken to be safely delivered to

The Source early the following morning and stored in the freezers there. Manna from heaven indeed! This kind of bounty is precious; the night shelter guests do not often eat fresh meat. Steve took a lot of chicken into the church freezer and various helpers from The Source managed to find some room in their home freezers too. I had just a few days earlier managed to clear a shelf in our own freezer which I had been hoping to use for Christmas food. Such is life!

The final task that has to be performed during in the season is that sleeping bags have to be washed regularly by a volunteer in a laundrette. I have done this, and have been involved in some interesting conversations with other customers.

Many people do not fully understand the need for night shelter provision until they are actually involved in some way. Then the work can become a passion, and very fulfilling. If for some reason I do not ever work in this kind of ministry again, I know that I have benefited enormously from my experiences, both spiritually and personally, and have experienced a greater sense of humility.

By now it should be apparent that the organisation of a night shelter is not for one church to accomplish alone, unless they perhaps open once a week. In order to have enough volunteers, the ministry must be shared between several churches, which can provide different venues and enough people. Even then, by the end of seven months or so, the volunteers need a break over the summer. If a trailer is involved, finding enough drivers is not always easy, partly because they need a tow bar to be fixed to their car, and partly because it is a huge responsibility: without the equipment in the trailer, the ministry cannot operate at all. This is not a difficult task, but it is a long-term commitment, so ideally a team of four or five could share the load more easily. If the night shelter is held just in one venue, of course this ceases to be a need.

Making big plans for God: prayerful preparation

A night shelter needs a period of special intercession in preparation. What might seem at first to be too large a task can be accomplished in God's timing and with the right preparation, not only of the practicalities, but also of our own hearts. The intercessors need to choose to believe the work is possible, to overcome fears and to trust God for every step, to pray for the corporate unity of the churches and for a heart of mission and love for the people they seek to serve. People with prophetic gifts are vitally important, to discern the right time to begin a ministry of this scale; prayer combined with fasting may be the way to start, to seek God's will. Also, there is the need to trust God when nothing seems to be happening, or when He seems to be giving strange instructions, or when external officialdom seems to be a problem.

We need to exercise our faith, however small it seems, and to believe that God will bring His plans to fruition. We may need to wait for God to speak, as the first disciples did before they received the Holy Spirit (Acts 2). We need to ask the presence of God to come to individuals in the churches, and the Holy Spirit to equip us with the generosity of love and perseverance that we need. We need to leave our comfort zone.

Hosting a Christmas tree witness

Most indoor shopping centres contain a large Christmas tree in December. I suggest first praying for an opportunity and then talking to the manager of your local centre. They may be glad of some innovative ideas to attract people to the centre, or at least to create a talking point.

If any church receives a God-given opportunity to host anything like this, it may be helpful to have some practical guidance points. The tree itself may be the one that stands in the shopping centre every year, or it may be necessary to make one.

The next need is to find volunteers to cut out cardboard stars large enough to write a prayer on. We also made smaller stars in silver card for people to write the name of a loved one in memoriam. There are various websites where large amounts of gold or silver card can be purchased. It would be very helpful to organise the making of your stars well in advance, even starting in the summer. One church asked their young people to help out.

The stars should, ideally, be of good-quality, shiny card so that they look fantastic when tied to the tree. In addition, they should be threaded and securely tied with coloured ribbon looped long enough for the customers to hang them easily from the branches. It is vital to produce stars that look good, not shoddy or cheap. If finances allow, it may be possible for some churches to buy some ready-made ones; we made our own because we do not have the finances and because it is also a way of involving some housebound elderly folk who would like to be involved and are not able to actually attend the tree.

The people who put effort into making the stars also prayed about the ministry and generated interest in it; there was a real buzz in some of the churches about it.

Some basic equipment is needed to establish a 'station', similar to equipment that might be used at a conference or an exhibition. We have some roll-up banners that we used as screens round our table when it was not in use, and a display board with a nativity picture and a poster to show what we were doing: 'Place a prayer star on the tree; it's free.' On the table we had a box of sweets for children, a box of stars, clipboards and pens, tissues and leaflets detailing all the Christmas church services in the town over the period. We also kept a notebook for any personal requests people made for ongoing prayer, or to make a note of particular stories.

We printed some basic guidelines for the volunteers at the tree concerning the best way to approach people, not to use Christian jargon, and so on, particularly if people had not done this kind of witness before (see Appendix 2).

We were fortunate in that we were able to use some chairs from the coffee shop next door, although generally we did not have time to sit down. By the end of the first week the lower part of the tree was so full of stars that we had to return one evening with a ladder and rehang them nearer the top to make room for the following week.

The best and busiest part of the day needs to be prioritised in terms of volunteers. We tend to find that there are fewer shoppers earlier in the day. Staffing the tree station is not hard once people catch the vision, and it is necessary to determine a sensible shift-length. We decided on three hours per shift and two or three people per shift from across the churches. This will, of course, be determined by the opening hours of the shopping centre.

As already mentioned, we did not feel it right to collect money through this witness. This alone sets it apart from many other events and speaks of God's love, which is free. However, it is up to the individual church or organisation to determine the right policy for itself.

Expect varied responses from the public. Some people want someone to talk to; one man came back several times just to have a chat. Some were upset and had very deep hurts; these people needed extra time and prayer. Some just wanted to know where they could attend a service in the town. Do expect God to surprise you and challenge you, and perhaps to humble you as you realise the extent of the spiritual need in your area and the richness of His grace for those who believe.

Easter Garden

There are many ways to make some sort of Easter display. Ours was constructed from a polystyrene sheet attached to a wooden base, and covered with a green fake-grass texture. We found the second year that wooden barbecue skewers stuck well into the polystyrene to support the card flower-heads. The first year we had bought some plastic green stems which, although they had a pointed end, did not always fix into the base very well.

Questions for reflection

1. Have you ever experienced a situation in which the rules have to be set aside in order to alleviate a difficult situation? Was it a difficult decision?

2. Could you approach your local shopping centre director and ask to run some kind of Easter weekend or Christmas 'stall' at which you could offer prayer and give out treats?

3. Does your local Council have a night shelter? Could your churches meet together to provide one for a season?

Fourteen
Where do we go from here?

In the first few weeks of 2018, there were further exciting developments at The Source and new contacts with different agencies. Amanda was approached by a representative of the Department of Work and Pensions, and they have provided an outreach worker to visit once a week. He provides advice with benefits and help with job-seeking for our guests.

The Job Centre has approached us to offer some fundraising. We may get short-term work placements for some of our clients in partnership with the Job Centre. The local college has asked if they can send some students to volunteer at The Source, offering free haircuts to the guests. Another unexpected offer is from a local dentist who has offered to provide free dental screening and advice at a weekly drop-in.

All these contacts have seemingly come from nowhere, but we know that God is bestowing favour on The Source and using it to further His work in the town. It is truly amazing what possibilities our Father God will open up as we are faithful in doing His work.

Another surprising occurrence is that some of the Pit Stop guests have asked for opportunities to do voluntary work in the shopping centre, or perhaps in other places, because they feel thankful for all the service they have received. This may, in time, be another opportunity for a project in the community.

In May 2018 Mick had another meeting with the director of the Vicarage Field shopping centre. At that meeting Mick was told that the centre would be open for another three years (there had been some question about this), and so he could offer The Source another rent-free three years, if we could still find the staff.

We now want to ensure that The Source is not so entirely taken over by Pit Stop and perceived as a place for the homeless, but has a wider focus. Mick has a plan to establish a network of community care, called the Christian Care Community Network, which will use The Source as its base. The Source will signpost people to give them an opportunity to link with a wider range of various networks, including possible prayer networks such as for the local police force. We explain more about the Network in more detail below.

Living in a London borough, we are very conscious of existence of the 'poor' around us, and their circumstances. Families are often large, sometimes living in small houses with few rooms. There are many unemployed, and people who are on low incomes, and some who have to maintain two jobs. There are many single-parent families, many of whom are not necessarily financially poor but who are struggling with another precious resource: time to share between working and caring for children.

God loves the poor. This is evident many times in Scripture, from the writings of Isaiah and other Old

Testament prophets through to the New Testament Gospels, the words of Jesus and the letters of Paul.

In the parable of the great banquet, Jesus tells of a man who invited many people to a great banquet, but they all made their excuses and did not come. So He ordered his servant, 'Go out quickly into the streets and alleys of the town and bring in the poor, the crippled, the blind and the lame' (Luke 14:21). If we do this, says Jesus, we 'will be blessed' (Luke 14:14).

At the beginning of His ministry, Jesus quotes from the prophet Isaiah: 'The Spirit of the Lord is on me, because he has anointed me to proclaim good news to the poor' (Luke 4:18). Jesus also said, 'Come to me, all you who are weary and burdened, and I will give you rest' (Matthew 11:28).

Jesus Himself was born into a relatively poor family, His earthly father being a carpenter by trade. Jesus had no money; He and His disciples wandered around, presumably eating at the homes of friends and people they spoke to in the towns they visited, or perhaps cooking their own food, barbecue-style. We read of Him producing a coin from the mouth of a fish to illustrate a point about money and taxes (Matthew 17:27); He did not reach into His pocket for His wallet.

Jesus lived among the poor all His life; He never had any riches of this world: house, money, possessions. When He crossed the Sea of Galilee, it was in a borrowed boat (Mark 4:35-36). When He rode into Jerusalem it was on a borrowed donkey (Matthew 21:1-11). He died on a cross like a criminal, and when He was buried, it was in a borrowed tomb (Matthew 27:57-60).

In the New Testament we see the kind of people He reached out to: people such as a blind beggar (Mark 10:46-52), a man with leprosy (Matthew 8:1-4), a woman with lots of broken relationships (John 4:1-42), a dishonest tax collector – the type of man who was hated by society (Luke 19:1-10).

One of the tasks carried out by the leaders of the early church was to distribute food to the widows in the community (Acts 6:1-7). In the Greco–Roman world, widows held a lowly position in the community and many had literally nobody to provide food for them. The new thinking in the early Christian church was the beginning of a proper care system for these and other 'outcasts' of society. If the Bible is our blueprint for social action, we should be also working in the community to meet needs.

If the churches are to see more of God's blessings, we as members of the church need to have God's compassion and love for the poor, vulnerable and broken-hearted people living in our neighbourhoods. This can only be done through our working together to provide services to help. Our ministries have therefore had a focus on helping: the Kidz Klub, the night shelter, The Source. In other areas, poverty and unemployment may not be the overriding concerns. Yet people living in wealthier areas still need to know the love of Jesus in their circumstances.

The Christian Care Community Network

A successful society is based on the operation and successful interaction of eight key areas: law and order, family life, education, social welfare, health service provision, politics, media and entertainment, and economy and business. All of these areas of society are vital, and all need discerning prayer support, to be held up to God in intercessory prayer. Several of these areas could form the basis of a united churches prayer time in themselves. Taking the example of education, the churches could pray for every church member working in education, for every school, for the staff, the discipline, the creativity needed in delivering a rigid curriculum, the children's protection and welfare, and so on.

In Barking, every charity is automatically given an 80 per cent business rate relief. Traditional churches receive all of this rate relief, but other churches may in the future be charged an additional 20 per cent or more if they are not seen to be contributing to society as a whole. Councils are now beginning to charge churches the full business rate on their premises if they do not appear to be serving the community in any way without profit to themselves. They see some churches charging for the hire of the church hall, or perhaps running a café for the church's own profit, which indicates a business venture.

Therefore, it is useful to conduct a survey of every church, to discover what they are doing in terms of outreach or service to the local area, without profit, whether it is running a parent and toddler group, for example, or a drop-in session for the elderly, or perhaps a youth club.

Many churches do not work together in their attempts to perform community services, leading to uncoordinated thinking and an individualistic approach. BCU is endeavouring to draw together all the activities the churches are working in across the borough to coordinate them. In this way, the Council or other body will have fewer individuals to deal with when consulting with the churches and investigating their social ministries.

The concept of the Christian Care Community Network has been one which Mick believes God has laid on his heart for some time. Mick has identified certain core areas of concern, such as family, health, education, social, and so on, from the above-mentioned key areas of society, and listed some of their possible subsections. For example, within the context of family can be found marriage, child support and youth support. Breaking this down further, child support can include the following needs: safety and security, meals, clothing, special needs and parenting.

Current activities to support these areas may include the local Scout group, Boys' Brigade, the Food Bank, a clothes bank. If child abuse were to be disclosed, it would, of course, need to be dealt with by professionals, and the relevant agencies should be called in to help. Churches might consider providing free parent support groups, homework or after-school clubs, or parent support groups for young or single parents. All of these areas are also concerns for prayer, either in a general way or for specific individuals who are befriended by the church members in a social support setting.

This kind of networking structure can be extended to all the eight key areas mentioned above. Churches can be encouraged to try to fill the gaps that are evident in the local setting, and to supply the extra dimension of prayer support.

CHRISTIAN CARE COMMUNITY NETWORK

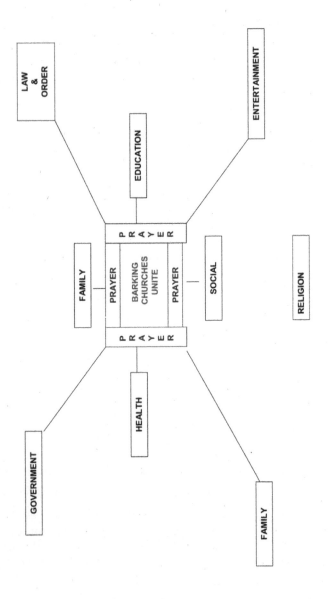

The Network is a plan for the future, and it will depend largely on the cooperation of churches working together and on excellent communication networks. As Council funding becomes more and more scarce, so the window of opportunity for the churches will open. The question is, if the churches do not respond, who will?

There are some places where a lot of these projects are well under way. For example, some food banks already run additional facilities to support families in need. Ideally, a network such as this one would need one specific location from which to operate, and, for us, it is hoped that The Source will initially be that place.

God loves the wealthy

In a more affluent town there will be people with different needs, not necessarily financial ones. There will be some who are seriously ill, or they may have fractured family relationships. There will be people struggling with loneliness and isolation. Young people may be bored or restless, perhaps partly because both parents have to work long hours to support the expenses of an affluent lifestyle. A more affluent area may not necessarily have available work for these young people, and they may be bored or aimless. We know from the media that alcoholism has been rising among our young people, both unemployed and young professionals.

Churches in these areas can do much to help in some of these situations. They would need to work together across the denominations to truly make a difference, and to put in place organised structures and teams of people, as well as prayer warriors, as already illustrated.

A united churches organisation may be able to provide a youth café or club, a games club or sports club, or a centre to help job-seekers. It may be able to open a lunchtime club for the elderly. A bereavement support group may be another ongoing need. Church buildings are great ready-made resources in which to host some of these ministries, ideally free of charge. In providing these ministries we can then share the gospel.

There may be other opportunities to gather people together in the community in these kinds of areas. The churches may be able to open their doors or find a building to host a leisure club such as a photography group, a music appreciation society or a book club. Social outings could be arranged to visit places of interest. In this way, people in the churches could build friendships with people within the community, through the medium of common interests. Gardening, crafts, theatre visits: all are opportunities for like-minded people to get together. There are conservation projects and tasks to be done in many areas to preserve wildlife.

We could add more ideas, as we look around us. God has put Christians in communities to be a witness of His love, and He will show us various creative ways to do this if we ask Him. Any community activity that the churches can provide, working across the denominations, will make a powerful statement about God's love.

Questions for reflection

1. Do you regularly have a personal encounter with God and experience His grace?

2. Does your united churches organisation have a vision for the future?

3. Is this written down and is it being prayed about?

4. Do you feel compassion for the poor?

5. What can you do in your town to help alleviate its difficulties?

6. Are there enough social networks in the town to cater for each age group?

7. Is there an opportunity to provide some kind of social group?

Fifteen
The challenge to the churches

There are many different styles of church today across the denominations, and many varied styles within the same denominations. Some churches use the formal structure of liturgy and the church calendar, and traditional music, while others use multimedia devices and modern music and are not bound by any formal structure. In the more-traditional churches the people can expect a consistent worship style and a structured service length with the same components, week by week. This brings about a sense of security and familiarity and provides a place where the people can anticipate a welcome, familiar faces and times of quiet reflection.

Other churches are not bound by church calendars, liturgy and structure, but they too provide a consistent and familiar worship style; perhaps the music is modern and includes large instrumental groups, and the service structure is also predetermined and structured, largely with the same components each week.

Both these types of church can be encouraging their members to be developing an intimate relationship with God. Conversely, they might simply be letting the people 'go through the motions' of religious activity each week without the church attendance affecting their heart.

A 'kingdom' church could be said to be one that encourages the people to develop a close relationship with God and teaches them to apply this to their lives, thus producing an effective witness to non-Christians.

A 'religious' church could be said to be one where the religious activity is of primary importance, with less emphasis on intimacy with God. Social action may come from this kind of church as a part of its regular activity, but without communicating the need for a relationship with Jesus.

Churches can be inward looking, welcoming those who fit in, the people having an attitude of personal gain and what the church can do for 'me'. There may be a sense of self-pursuit ('ours is the best church in town'), self-sufficiency, even perhaps a gospel of entertainment. Success is based on pleasing and making the congregation happy, and the upkeep of the building is of high priority.

A kingdom-style approach focuses on a life rooted in a relationship with God. This type of church will naturally be more outward focused, more adaptable to being able to accommodate all kinds of people, less bound by tradition. It will be open to the guidance of the Holy Spirit in its planning, and ready to implement change.

Jesus did not ask us to tell people what they are doing wrong. He asked us to love them. Love is personal. It requires an embrace, a hug. It is about understanding God's grace. It is difficult to carry grace if you haven't had an encounter with the Giver of grace. First, we must experience Him. Second, we must understand who we truly are: that we are loved. Then we are in a better position to share that love with others.

A church operating with more of a kingdom focus will be people focused rather than building focused. It will use its building for the community where possible, perhaps ministering to the poor in a town, perhaps by running a lunchtime club, or getting involved in a food bank.

A kingdom spirit lives by faith. Faith does not operate in the realm of the possible. Faith begins where human power ends. Charles, the leader of our night shelter, has at times had to believe God for finances in order to keep the shelter open, acting in faith that God would provide. We can read accounts of many other Christian ministry leaders having to do the same thing. God is calling us to choose faith, even when we don't know what is on the other side. Our human nature is to be in control and to fear for uncertainties.

We should not have a 'bless me' mentality, but a 'bless others and the local community' mentality. Jesus lived and worked in the towns and the streets. He did not have a building to operate from, because that would have rooted Him in one place. He spent very little time in synagogues. To have a kingdom of God mindset is to have a mindset that looks outward to the needs of people.

Jesus said, 'Very truly I tell you, whoever believes in me will do the works I have been doing, and they will do even greater things than these, because I am going to the Father' (John 14:12).

Some Christians have been able to perform 'signs and wonders', some of the 'works' of Jesus; perhaps healing people by praying for them, or speaking out a word from God that will guide them. This is only possible when we have a close relationship with Jesus and can feel God giving us a special prompting to act.

Working outside the box

Over the seven years we have been running BCU we have often been in despair over the apparent indifference by many church leaders and members towards the work we are doing. So many churches focus on their own programmes, to the exclusion of all outside organisations. Mick has sometimes mentioned this to leaders, and their very reasonable answers are that the running of their church is their primary responsibility and they are called to look after the spiritual welfare of the people in their congregations. One leader said, 'I will only help those who come through the church door; I have no time or resources to help anyone outside.'

Jesus, the Good Shepherd, went looking for the lost sheep (John 10:11; Luke 15:3-6).

Another church leader told Mick that his job is to look after the spiritual well-being of the members of his congregation and to keep them happy, to equip them to grow in biblical knowledge and spiritual experience so that they will be able to reach out with the gospel to people during the week.

This kind of statement, while on the face of it is an admirable aim, may not ultimately encourage the church members as a whole to be outward looking to serve the community in which the church has a presence. This minister is also assuming that the members will do as he suggests, whereas if the church leadership were to actively promote some of the ministries we are running, the people would have a chance to make up their own minds whether to be involved or not. Those members who are indeed, as he suggests, working to bring people to faith in their workplaces and home situations, probably do so, whereas other people might be glad of an opportunity to become involved in a ministry that is already operating. They would also have the joy of making new friends from churches of other denominations and outlooks, thereby widening their awareness of the way other people experience and outwork their Christian faith. We have seen this happen many times as Christians from different churches have made deep and meaningful friendships with like-minded people they would not have otherwise met.

Our experience over the last seven years has been that if a church leadership steps out in faith and allows a higher profile of or actively promotes the work a united group does in the community, the church members who get involved benefit and grow in their Christian faith and excitement so much that they are better equipped to contribute to the activities in their own church, as well as seeing the value of any community outreach the church is doing.

One church vicar told us that the active involvement in and hosting of the night shelter in her church made a huge difference to the enthusiasm of the members of her congregation in this and in other areas of church life. She was very enthusiastic about the venture and a great supporter of BCU ministries.

Some churches have a somewhat limited idea of what constitutes 'outreach' to the local community. If they host a daily playgroup, a weekly keep-fit session or a craft afternoon they think they are doing enough to make the church accessible to those outside it. All these things are legitimate activities and do provide a service but, sadly, sometimes the churches are charging money to the users of these activities, and thus are actually running a business venture in the eyes of the community or the local Council, rather than helping the community for free.

God's love is free, and if we as Christians and churches can provide something for free, this is a very good witness to those outside, because everyone expects to pay for everything. In the early days of The Source we ran a weekly activity club for elderly people. It was a surprise to the attendees that everything was free, and this made a very positive statement about God's love. (Sadly, this activity was curtailed after a few months owing to the lack of interest by the residents, but one or two of the users of the club maintained an ongoing relationship with The Source staff by coming regularly to see us.)

Who are we trying to reach?

It is sometimes said that the church as an organisation is 'too middle class'. The churches of any particular town should be able to encourage people of all walks of life to attend on Sundays or come along to the midweek activities, or send their children to the children's club or youth club. However, sometimes the people who run such activities are somewhat blinkered and accustomed to the same type of people attending, often people who are like themselves.

Once Mick was talking to a church member about the proposed night shelter ministry and the question was asked, 'What if a homeless person were to come to our service? What would we do?' Mick's reaction was one of surprise, but he just told the questioner that a homeless person is no different from anyone else and should be treated accordingly.

There is a memorable, true tale of a new church minister who disguised himself as a homeless tramp and attended a service in the church of which he was about to become the leader. He was largely ignored and treated with indifference. Halfway through the morning service he removed his disguise and introduced himself as the new minister, to the horror and embarrassment of all.[10]

We need to be flexible, open to all and welcoming, even if visitors do not know the expected norms of church attendance: to be quiet during the delivery of the sermon, to sit and stand appropriately, and so on. New people need to feel at ease, and will probably need a lot of explanation about what is occurring and why we do certain things.

At times there can be too much head knowledge and not enough heart compassion. In some churches there is an excellent programme of biblical teaching and the congregation members are well grounded in theology. Week after week we sit and listen to well-researched and well-delivered sermons. But all this teaching is of little or no relevance to outsiders, who need to see God's love in

---

[10] Source unknown.

action and to hear how it relates to their own situations. We need to apply the teaching that we have received to our lives, and to help others understand the relevance of God's call.

The need for corporate prayer

All our best efforts and ideas will have little effect in reaching the community without an organised and ongoing prayer strategy. In this it is also necessary to wait in silence to hear God speak. He may do this clearly in a word, or give someone an impression in their spirit over a period of time. He will usually repeat it and speak to more than one person, to confirm the word or impression. Once this has been weighed against Scripture and with others, we can determine when it is the right time to begin a ministry, or who the best person to lead it may be. God may be instructing us to do something unexpected or surprising; sometimes He leads us to make contact with someone outside the church or in another organisation who can help with money, equipment or space.

We also require hearts to care for needy people, and only God can give us enough of His compassion to enable us to work successfully over a long time. This compassion comes through much prayer and a sense of humility before God.

In early 2018 I chatted to Michael Taylor, one of the BCU trustees. Michael has worked in The Source for seven months, several times a week, and he has become passionate about the work there. He serves the Pit Stop guests in many ways, including devising delicious soups from whatever tins of beans, pulses and vegetables we happen to have in store each week.

I asked Michael about what he sees is the primary purpose of church unity.

'To fulfil the purpose of the words in Jesus' prayer in John's Gospel [John 17], so that in our unity the world will know of our love for each other and God's love for people. Individuals can work together but churches as institutions are often more inflexible with rules and structures, and so on.'

I asked him how he has seen this love in action in The Source.

'People from different denominations all work for the common good of helping people. It is only working together that brings us together, otherwise we would not know each other.'

Has working in The Source given Michael any special revelation of God's character and the way He works?

Michael told me how he has seen God's supernatural provision of food on occasions when we have run out. On a day we are short of bread, for example, a member of a local company will come to the door of The Source to offer us their surplus bread resulting from a mistake in their administration system, when someone ordered too much. 'This confirms that what we are doing is correct, and stops the prospect of the enemy enjoying us running out of food.'

Michael also says he has been much challenged over having to use lots of patience in The Source – a challenge common to all of us.

Michael has been struck by the simple fact of how sometimes saying a prayer before the meal at The Source can be a powerful thing that speaks of the simplicity of our faith, and how the guests have commented on this non-complicated way of prayer.

'We pontificate too much and make religious speeches,' says Michael.

What made Michael want to become a trustee?

Michael saw it as an opportunity to do something to help the less fortunate, that this was a ministry opportunity and can be a form of evangelism. He cited the example of God telling Moses to 'order them [the Israelites] to get moving', when Moses led the people across the divided Red Sea (Exodus 14:15-16, *The Message*).

Lack of money and the call of God to the churches

The principle of working together and receiving God's favour may apply to financial commitment. We have asked the churches all to give us a small, regular donation each month to support the ministries. Very few have done so, and as a result we are struggling to keep some of them going. Many churches willingly send money overseas in regular support of missionaries they have not seen for years – and it is right that they do so – yet they are unable to give any money to a mission happening in their own town, involving people in their own church. This seems extremely ironic, to say the least. Sometimes churches do not financially support either local ministries or those elsewhere in the country.

We are at the moment contemplating employing a professional fundraiser to apply for grants to keep the night shelter and The Source operating. Everyone is hard pressed these days, but we believe that the biblical principle of God rewarding a generous giver applies as much to the united churches as a body as it does to individuals within the churches.

For a detailed study of what comprises a kingdom people and a kingdom church, see Appendices 4 and 5.

Questions for reflection

1. Does your church open its doors during the week and freely serve the community?

2. Do your church members feel free to work alongside members of other local churches and work in their ministries?

3. Would your church consider diverting money to help in a local mission?

4. Jesus wept over Jerusalem (Luke 19:41); He really cared about the needs of the people. Do we cry over the people in our town?

Sixteen
Obstacles to church unity

There may be some who, having read so far, will be thinking, 'That's all very well for them in Barking, but my situation is very different.' Some church leaders may very reasonably object that there are no 'one size fits all' strategies, and that every group of churches, and each church, has its own specific character.

Barking is not a particularly important or out-of-the-ordinary town, but we believe that we have been privileged to have been shown a way forward by God Himself, and BCU as an organisation has tried to the best of its ability to follow His leading. I believe that this can happen to any group of churches who are genuinely seeking to reach their community as a united body.

We will now look at some common perceived obstacles and objections that may prevent churches working together. Then in the following chapter we will take each obstacle in turn to discover whether they can be overcome, referring to Scripture to shed further light. These hypothetical objections could be reasons why church leaders are reluctant to promote the activities of an organisation of united churches.

Objection 1: 'I don't have the time.'

The pressure of work both on the solitary vicar/leader and on the pastor who has a team to work with is very great. They have to be all things to all members of the congregation, and this comprises many groups of people. A church congregation is a microcosm of a whole society. A school head teacher has to deal primarily with three sets of people: teachers, pupils and parents, and the common concern of all is good education. A pastor, on the other hand, is liaising with families, the lonely, the elderly, young people and children, and trying to maintain the interest and engagement of people in many walks of life, be they health workers, teachers, business workers or owners, manual workers or the unemployed. In short, there is a whole community of people inside the church to deal with, without looking outside for another set of people.

A church leader has many responsibilities, especially if they are the only one, without a team to work with. The leader may even have a full-time secular job. We have found that ministers can sometimes not prioritise or even engage with the work of BCU because their time seems to be so completely taken up with running their churches and responding to the pastoral needs of the people therein. Then there are all the administrative responsibilities: filling in forms to comply with legislation, budgeting, looking after the building, and other matters. On top of this, there are the meetings of different types to prepare for and the all-important weekly sermon.

Objection 2: 'I am exhausted.'

This is closely allied to objection number one. The church pastor, of all people, needs times of spiritual refreshment and to be able to recharge their spiritual 'batteries', to pray and seek God's face for them personally and for the church, to receive wisdom and guidance. This is likely to be a rare occurrence if there is no leadership team to relieve the pastor of regular weekly responsibilities. The hidden side of a pastor's work is that of spending much time in prayer, and this may become side-lined at times because of the demands of the public duties. Any hard-pressed pastor is likely to jettison the opportunity of extra united churches events if they are suffering from burnout.

Objection 3: 'My priority has to be about church attendance.'

This is a really difficult and demanding issue. It may be that the head office of a denomination requires a weekly tally of 'bums on seats', thus making the issue a significant one for the leader. Also, the regular congregation members often bring in a significant amount of the money that is needed to run the church. The success of a church has traditionally been measured by its numerical size. In many walks of life, such as entertainment, retail, project leading and business, the success of a venture is measured by how many people attend the event, buy the product or follow the idea put forward. The church is sometimes no different, in that a high level of attendance gives the appearance of success. The delivery of the sermon, therefore, becomes of significant importance.

Traditionally, even in the world outside the church, the minister's first responsibility is to be seen to preach a good sermon. This is the public face of the church, the 'entertainment factor' which people are quick to judge. 'Nice sermon, vicar,' is the phrase heard, perhaps almost as often as the 'More tea, vicar?' phrase of public entertainment. These phrases suggest that the two primary responsibilities of the vicar are to preach an entertaining and interesting sermon and to visit the sick and housebound regularly. Some church members have even left churches because they have not been visited at home by church leaders when they felt they needed to be, or because the sermons have not been to their taste.

Both these activities portray a comfortable, non-confrontational task but they are, in reality, sometimes disproportionately important. A vicar or pastor may therefore spend a large part of their time in the week writing a sermon, perhaps with a PowerPoint presentation, to present an entertaining and challenging talk. This is important, but perhaps too much time is sometimes allocated to the task.

Objection 4: 'My church members may become wrongly influenced.'

This is an interesting objection, because it can be seen to indicate an insecurity in the mind of the objector. Some church leaders may be afraid that, in mixing with those of other denominations, congregation members may become 'led astray' or confused by encountering different theological points of view.

Pressure may be on a leader to conform to the different tenets of their denomination, to uphold its traditions, to obey the authority laid down by the denominational head office. Some doctrinal issues are, indeed, important and crucial to the underlying beliefs of the Christian church. But there are others that could easily be laid aside with no animosity or discussion needed. For example, baptism is a command of Jesus, and surely relevant in all forms. There are many things that unite us, and there are some issues that people in different denominations approach differently; it is better to focus on the work in hand than on the potential issues that would divide us.

Objection 5: 'It's my church and we have spent a lot of money on the building.'

The building and its upkeep and maintenance can become an obsession, and assume an importance that seems out of proportion. The church has just had an expensive kitchen fitted. The new carpets must not be marked. The newly restored stained-glass windows must be protected.

In our contacts with different churches, both in Barking and other towns, we have seen many examples of this kind of possessiveness about church buildings. It is sometimes a reason that a church is not made available to the general public, or used to help the homeless or perhaps to host a children's group. One church refused to host the night shelter because the leaders were afraid of damage to the pews or carpets. The appearance of the sanctuary must be maintained, kept clean and undisturbed. I was once fascinated to see a church leader actually measuring the distance between the chairs with a ruler before a service, presumably so that they looked neat from his point of view. Whatever would he do, I mused, if anyone were to actually sit in them or move them an inch or two?

As a contrast to this, we have seen one or two churches in central London that remain open all day in winter in order to host any homeless people who need shelter, and it is the sanctuary itself that is available. Another church hosts a coffee and sandwich bar where office workers can enjoy lunch. Visitors are invited to receive prayer at the same time if they would like to.

Objection 6: 'My church members may become distracted or leave.'

This objection is similar to number 4, in that it may indicate a sense of insecurity in the church leader. Some leaders are nervous about their members associating too much with Christians in other churches because they are afraid that their members might be more attracted to another church.

I was once talking to a leader and proposing to recruit some church members to start a Companions ministry to those outside the church. I met with a refusal to allow me to do so, on the grounds that he wanted me to visit people in the church instead, this being the immediate need that he was concerned with. Fortunately, this is the only time I have personally encountered this type of overtly narrow thinking, but sadly we have heard of other people in churches who have been discouraged in their community ministries instead of encouraged. This surely contradicts the words of the Great Commission (Matthew 28:18-20) to 'Go'.

The command by Jesus was to 'Go and make disciples of all nations, baptising them in the name of the Father and of the Son and of the Holy Spirit, and teaching them to obey everything I have commanded you' (Matthew 28:19-20). These words are very familiar, but many church leaders still seem to want people to 'Come' to the church.

In centuries past people did, indeed, come; church attendance was a normal weekly activity. In those days Christianity was part of school education and most people held to a belief in the Christian God and the Christian religion, with all its accepted norms of behaviour and standards of what was right and wrong. Now our culture has completely changed, with many different faiths being seen as acceptable and given equality of freedom and importance. Christianity is only one of many religions in Great Britain today, and most children are not brought up with any Christian knowledge. People are, as we know, not attending church, and so the church needs to have a different approach to evangelism. To engage with people's needs and to meet them outside the four walls of the church is the only way to introduce them to Jesus.

Jesus never operated from within the church. He was on the streets, among the people where they were, in the marketplace and in their homes. These are places where we currently have the freedom to go with the gospel. We, as His church, should be making the most of every opportunity to do so.

Despondency

In many walks of life, once the initial enthusiasm for a venture has worn off, it is difficult to maintain a consistent momentum to keep a project going, particularly if it is staffed by volunteers. We have found this to be the case in our ministries, and have had times when the prayer meetings are poorly attended, and church members have been more reticent than previously.

If we were all really concerned about the needy people in our town and we regularly interceded for the poor and needy and for the lost, we would probably maintain a more compassionate heart for people. In order to do this, we need to call on the Holy Spirit to fill us with the love of Jesus daily. We all have such busy lives, with many calls on our time, particularly if we have families and demanding jobs.

Do we look around us at the faces of the people we pass in the street? Do we notice if our neighbour has a need? Do we always leave the volunteering to somebody else? It is easy to become bored, disinterested or apathetic, particularly if we are in a long-term ministry such as The Source, or perhaps helping to run the Kidz Klub. Sadly, sometimes because people are volunteers in a ministry, the commitment to attend is not as strong as it might be if they were paid to work there. Volunteers may have the attitude that it doesn't matter if they are late, or if they decide to cancel at the last minute, because, after all, other people will help, and they are not being paid to turn up. This can sometimes jeopardise the smooth running of a ministry, because it cannot operate without the expected core staff.

Too much pressure is then brought to bear on the existing volunteers, and they in turn may become disillusioned and stop coming to help. A downward spiral is thereby created. In the apostle Paul's letter to the Corinthians he writes, 'Now it is required that those who have been given a trust must prove faithful' (1 Corinthians 4:2).

We need to mentally put ourselves in the place of the people we are trying to help, be they the service users or other volunteers. We also need to have realistic expectations of our own abilities and time commitments. For this reason it would be really useful to have two teams of workers who can work alternately, one week on and one week off, or month by month, or sometimes to recruit someone from an outside agency to help for a while, as we did with Luis. This can bring a relief to the existing team, and also provide cover for inevitable sickness or other needs.

Question for reflection

Do your church members or leaders identify with any of these objections?

Seventeen
Objections answered: the call to unity

Objection 1: 'I don't have the time.'

This is a problem for nearly everyone who is in any kind of employment. It may seem an insurmountable problem, and needs to be approached with prayer and creative thinking. It is certain that the hard-pressed church leader would not have time to engage with all activities and ministries such as the ones we have mentioned so far, but it is to be hoped that they would at least be able to select one or two which appeal to their interests.

It may be that, for a leader, although attending a prayer meeting, for example, may seem like part of their work, something else could be exchanged if necessary, perhaps moved to another day, to free up the time in order for them to at least be able to find out what is happening in the united churches body. (At some of our united prayer meetings the whole range of activities have been discussed, reported on and prayed for.) In this way, the leader may become interested in a particular ministry and decide to bring it to the attention of the church leadership team with a view to engaging with it as a church.

There may be several members of a church who are gifted in a particular field, such as cooking, and so perhaps the church could become a centre for a night shelter or an elderly people's lunch club. This need not necessarily preclude the church members from being involved with other ministries, but means that the church might begin to specialise in a particular field.

Much prayerful preparation is needed by a church as a whole before taking on a long-term commitment of any kind, but it is important that the church is willing to look outside its four walls to the community. One church may become involved in a ministry just for a season; this is still a wonderful opportunity to serve and will bring great blessing to all involved.

> How good and pleasant it is
> when God's people live together in unity!
> [We might substitute 'work together'.]
> It is like precious oil poured on the head,
> running down on the beard ...
> For there the Lord bestows his blessing.
> *Psalm 133*

The picture of precious oil is a beautiful one, because the flow of oil is a continuous movement, and some oils are sweet-smelling. Oil also lubricates, makes smooth and enables something to operate smoothly. Another blessing for church leaders of working together is that meeting other church leaders can be a great support and encouragement.

Objection 2: 'I am exhausted.'

In order to take up a new project, something often has to be laid down. Again, this is a matter for prayer. God will show His people where their priorities should lie. It is often said, 'God will make a way where there seems to be no way,' and this principle can be applied to our time as well as to our resources or to other problems. It may be that the exhausted leader is doing many things to support the church, things that others should be doing. This may be because the leader has not identified the breadth of skills available within the congregation. Others within the church may have many gifts or talents to engage with tasks which the minister could delegate to them, thus freeing them to explore the ministries of united churches or to at least befriend other ministers in the town. For more on this, see Appendix 3: Talents profile. This is a tool to identify the range of gifts within the people of a church.

The whole issue of burnout among leaders is one that I am not qualified to address here, and I know that it is a difficult one. 'Time out' and retreat times are surely essential for a church leader, and, if necessary, they may need the help of other ministers or apostolic leaders in the area to facilitate these.

There may be a particular ministry that a church is finding it hard to facilitate alone, perhaps the running of a youth club, for example. A creative way to solve this might simply be to abandon the club and encourage the young people to join the club being run by the church down the road.

Objection 3: 'My priority has to be about church attendance.'

The issue of church attendance may be, as I have said, a pressing one, a visible one and sometimes a financial issue. However, we have to remember that, in God's economy, the biggest is not necessarily the best. Jesus wants His bride to be not necessarily big but beautiful inside. I am of the opinion that God is not so concerned with the number of worshippers attending a church as with the condition of their hearts and their love for Him. He wants church members to be always drawing closer to Him and to each other in order to reach those outside the church with the gospel. A church that is small in numbers can be used by God to do great things. We have found that sometimes the smaller churches have been the most supportive of our ministries.

Jesus said, 'A new command I give you: love one another. As I have loved you, so you must love one another. By this everyone will know that you are my disciples, if you love one another' (John 13:34-35).

Some churches have a very strong focus on good Bible teaching and preaching. This is very good, but then there may come a time when the church members need to put this teaching into practice in practical ways, including working outside the four walls of the church to reach the lost and those who are seeking.

When a church embarks on an evangelistic ministry, or simply one that provides a service to the community, people will inevitably be drawn into the church, perhaps out of curiosity or because of friendships that they have made with church members. This in itself will increase the church attendance.

Objection 4: 'My church members may become wrongly influenced.'

It is good and healthy for Christians of different denominations and viewpoints to join together in prayer and in work. We all worship and serve the same God, and we all want to see others come to faith. In Paul's letter to the Corinthians he writes of the church being represented as a body with different parts. This can be applied to a group of churches as well as to one church.

> Just as a body, though one, has many parts, but all its many parts form one body, so it is with Christ. For we were all baptised by one Spirit so as to form one body – whether Jews or Gentiles, slave or free …
> *1 Corinthians 12:12-13*

… or Baptists or Methodists or Pentecostals…

Although there are different emphases on doctrinal points and various methods of worship and church governance among the denominations, these issues should not and do not usually prevent Christians from making friendships and working together. We can learn a lot from each other, even because of our different traditions and emphases. I once had a friendship with a Roman Catholic boy who introduced me to the idea of setting aside set times of the day to pray, and to the use of candles as symbols and aids to worship. I forgot about our conversations after a while, but many years later I have been reminded of these valuable aids to connect with God and am more open to them.

Matters of theology don't seem to matter when we are washing dishes together in The Source. The way someone else worships using liturgy as opposed to the free-style church services I am more used to is of little significance when we are both trying to find ways of eking out the potatoes at the night shelter.

In BCU and, I am sure, in other united churches movements, lovely new friendships have been formed between Christians living in the same area or perhaps even the same street who were unaware of each other's faith before they met through the united church movement.

Objection 5: 'It's my church and we have spent a lot of money on the building.'

Whose church is it? Surely the church is God's, and His priority is people, not buildings. Of course, we have all been inspired to worship by being in a beautiful place, be it in a building or a forest or on a mountain. But the people of the early church met in each other's homes as well as in the temple courts (Acts 2:46). Jesus never taught us to build structures to close ourselves in and to keep others out.

There are, indeed, many beautiful cathedrals and other churches throughout the Christian world which contain works of art to inspire us to seek God in different ways. Whole books have been written about these, and they can provide an interesting study of the faith of the artists and their patrons throughout history. Conversely, and depressingly, there are a number of not-so-attractive churches which are very old and, although the people are welcoming, the buildings are cold and smell of damp for most of the year. One cannot help admiring the fortitude of the congregation for spending the required hour in them every week. It is often necessary to spend a great deal of money on these old churches to make them habitable. In my opinion, a church building should at least be warm and airy and have comfortable seating.

Be that as it may, the church building, although very precious to many members, is surely of secondary importance, and the preservation of certain features should not detract the church members from their primary mission: to accommodate the lost and those who are seeking God. The new carpets/kitchen/windows, etc, are a great asset to the building and are supposed to make life more convenient and comfortable for everyone, not just the church members. How would a restaurant stay open if the proprietors were nervous of anyone spilling anything on the new carpet?

Objection 6: 'My church members may become distracted or leave.'

Most Christians who have the desire to join a ministry in the town to reach the lost will be fully aware of their prior commitment to the activities of their own church. They may or may not be people who are responsible for the smooth running of a church activity. If they are, there must surely be found someone in the church who can step into that position and release the person. If this is not the case, then it is the responsibility of the individual to decide whether they can sensibly continue to be involved in both ministries. If necessary, the church member may feel that the call of God to serve outside the church is more urgent that the perceived need to stay.

God will guide everyone concerned if they pray about these issues, and He will bring new people forward to fill gaps in the workforce of a church ministry He wants to bless. Many churches will graciously release and commission their members to begin a new work in a united churches ministry and will then avidly follow its progress, just as they would a missionary they sent to Africa. After all, mission is still mission in one's home town.

Inside/outside

We in the church have a spiritual security of faith in and a relationship with a caring God, and, although our lives are fraught with the same problems as everyone else, we are conscious of a sense of belonging. We each have our own role to play in the operation of the church, or, if we have no specific operational tasks, we generally have our allotted position in the church's social structure, unless we happen to be a very new member.

The reality is that many church leaders are preoccupied with systems designed to facilitate the smooth running of their churches and prioritise the all-important weekly Sunday service above all other considerations. The very word 'service' should suggest to the church members that the priority of the church should be to serve those outside it, to look for opportunities to show God's love to people in practical ways.

This is where The Source has been such a wonderful, God-given opportunity to do this very thing.

We in BCU have sometimes been pleasantly surprised and thrilled when a small church, not rich in numbers or finances, has opened its doors to host the Megacities team, or a church has decided to make an unexpected donation to The Source or the night shelter. Another church welcomed the Music Academy when it needed to relocate, looking on the ministry as an opportunity to connect into the community.

To sum up, there are many different challenges here:

- ❖ Who owns our churches? Do they belong to the leaders or to God?

- ❖ The challenge to pray much before any action takes place, to listen to God's heart.

- ❖ The challenge for the church to be seen in the community, to be more visible through community projects, thereby potentially opening itself to criticism and misunderstanding, either from those in civil leadership or from others inside the church.

- ❖ The challenge not to be tempted to promise more than we can deliver; this is always difficult when we can see the extent of the need.

- ❖ The challenge for already hard-pressed churches to give some of their financial resources to a community ministry.

❖ The same challenge regarding time: hours to be diverted from a particular church ministry to a united churches ministry.

❖ The challenge for churches to look beyond their established, carefully planned programmes and agendas to incorporate new ideas or approaches, to fit in with the vision of different churches or organisations.

❖ The challenge to appoint a single representative or body to engage in civic partnership. Councils do not want to deal with a hundred church leaders.

❖ The challenge to set up a coordinated approach and strategy through a united church movement.

❖ To be willing to take risks for God.

If we can look outwards more, and towards the needs in the community, God can supply the ideas, the resources and the money to enable wonderful things to happen to draw people closer to Himself. We serve a great God who never fails to surprise us. Glory to His name!

Part Three

Resources Section

This part of the book contains examples of some practical leaflets and handouts which we have used to advise our volunteers.

1. Prayer diary

The monthly prayer diary is a supplementary resource which is sent to all the church leaders and given out at united prayer meetings and to anyone who wants one. In it are mentioned the local schools, any upcoming events, community ministries, churches and their leaders, and BCU ministries. We also include items of national concern.

2. Dos and don'ts at Christmas

This is a leaflet given to volunteers for the Christmas tree witness. It outlines basic advice and rules to enable the volunteers to be able to approach their contacts with caution and in a way that will enable both parties to feel natural and comfortable.

3. Serving God: Talents profile

This is a two-page leaflet questionnaire for individual church members, to help church leaders carry out an audit of the skills of their members and to help the members to reflect on their own abilities.

4. Being kingdom people

This leaflet enables church members to pray and think about their own spiritual growth, and to assess their progress in developing their relationship with God.

5. Being a kingdom church

This leaflet enables church leaders to reflect on and assess the church's spiritual progression and growth as a body over a short period of time, perhaps to compare its position from the last occasion when this was done.

6. Prophetic words

I have included here a selection of the prophecies we received in the early years. These were very motivational for us in helping us to see that God was truly guiding us in our ventures.

Appendix 1
Prayer diary

Barking Churches unite

PRAYER DIARY – July 2018

MONDAY	TUESDAY	WEDNESDAY	THURSDAY	FRIDAY
2 The SOURCE Amanda (Manager) Carol & Linda Vicarage Field Shopping Centre	3 Grace Ministries Paul A Eastbury School Eastbury Centre	4 Dagenham Civic Centre Councillors Mayor Leader of Council	5 Kings Church Leadership Team Upney Evangelism	6 Barking Churches Unite Vision & Trustees Mick Mednick
9 The SOURCE Vicarage Field Shopping Centre Night Shelter Venue Christ Church	10 United Prayer Meeting St Erkenwald 7.45pm Night Shelter Venue Barking Methodist	11 Barking Methodist Church Elders James K Night Shelter Venue Oxlow Lane Baptist	12 Christ Kingdom Church John B Night Shelter Bethel Church	13 Police Knife Crime Killings Night Shelter Venue Chadwell Heath Baptist
16 The SOURCE Amanda (Manager) Carol & Linda Business Chaplaincy in Vicarage Field	17 Elim Christian Centre Leadership Team Axe Street Estate Northbury Primary School, Barking & Dagenham Schools	18 St Patrick's Church Portuguese Group Spanish Group Mark K	19 St Patrick's Leadership Team Eastbury Manor Hs Eastbury School Eastbury Estate	20 Lyon Business Estate Barking Station Peace & safety Barking Park - Peace

Appendix 2
Dos and don'ts at Christmas and Easter

Vicarage Field Christmas Tree / Easter Garden Witness

Dos and don'ts

Dos – Before

❖ In the days before your shift, come before God to prepare your heart and mind.

❖ Pray together as a team at the start of your shift.

❖ If you are comfortable with meeting strangers, that's good, but if you are not, team up with those who are – this is an opportunity for growth.

❖ Pray the Commissioning Prayer at the start of your shift.

Dos – On your shift

❖ Ask the names of those who come for a star or flower

❖ Ask 'For what should I pray?'

❖ Ask 'Are you a Christian?'

❖ Listen to those before you *and* listen to God.

❖ Make your prayers brief.

- ❖ Pray discreetly.
- ❖ If they would prefer to sit, then sit alongside them.
- ❖ Be ready to help folk write their prayers out, summarising if necessary.
- ❖ Place the star/flower on the tree/garden together.
- ❖ Log book – be sensitive. Enter a sentence anonymously if appropriate.
- ❖ Give out BCU Christmas/Easter literature relating to church services.

Don'ts – On your shift

- ❖ No preaching – people have come to shop.
- ❖ Don't make assumptions.
- ❖ Don't insist on prayer. Let them go if they say 'no' but be receptive if they change their mind.
- ❖ Don't make promises.
- ❖ Don't give out your personal details.
- ❖ Don't request a donation.

Don'ts – After your shift

- ❖ Confidentiality – even if you are excited, don't share with others.

Dealing with conflict

In the unlikely event of conflict, Security is located on the top floor next door to The Source.

CONTACT PHONE NUMBER: xxxxxx

Commissioning Prayer

Father God,

As disciples of Jesus,

We accept our commission from You

To bless the lives of those we meet today.

Through the leading of Your Holy Spirit,

We pray for divine appointments,

Believing You for wisdom and courage

To boldly, yet gently, release the kingdom

Over all who choose to come.

Lord Jesus,

Release a greater anointing on us,

So Your glory radiates from within us for all to see.

May we truly be Your ambassadors

Today, always and everywhere.

Give us eyes to see,

Ears to hear and hearts to reach out

As we hear the cry of those You have ordained us to meet.

Father, Your Son, our Saviour Jesus Christ,

Modelled for us what it means to be a servant

Through washing the feet of His disciples.

May we exhibit that same servant attitude

Today, always and everywhere.

Thank you, Father,

That as we join our value system to Yours

And partner with heaven,

You shower Favour, Blessings and Increase upon us.

For Your glory, worthy Jesus.

Amen.

Appendix 3
Serving God: Talents profile

Name _____ Profession _____

Please rank as follows:
3 there is much evidence of this
2 there is some evidence of this
1 there are only a few signs of this.

Talents and skills

Skills	Rating	Skills	Rating
Administration		Caring for people	
Management		Creative – art, drama, writing, dance	
Teaching		Playing an instrument	
Youthwork		Driving/transport	
Children's work		DIY	
Cooking		Plumbing	
Baking		Electrical	
Talking		Car maintenance	
Listening		Decorating	
Singing		Building	
ICT		Organisation	

Calling and purpose

Gifting	Rating	Gifting	Rating
Teaching		Hospitality	
Prayer and intercession		Evangelism	
Serving the poor		Debt advice	
Leadership		Causes of justice and mercy	
Pastoring		Helping	
Youthwork		Befriending	
Children's work		Counselling	
Prison ministry		Administration	
Homeless ministry		Sport	

Community ministries interests

Interests	Rating	Interests	Rating
Street support		Business support	
Prayer		Hospital	
Night shelter/homeless		Debt and budget advice	
Elderly		Food bank	
Bereavement		Parenting	
Youth		Befriending	
Children		Counselling	
Prison		Mentoring	

Appendix 4 (For individual reflection) Being kingdom people

Serving God

God's heart is to reconcile the world to Himself in Jesus. As Christians we are called to be 'kingdom people'. We should be using our spiritual gifts, talents and callings in our daily lives to demonstrate God's love to the world. In this way we bring in God's presence where we go.

'The kingdom of God has come near. Repent and believe the good news!' (Mark 1:15).

As Christians, we are called to be agents of transformation in the world, according to God's loving purposes in Christ. The mission and ministry of the church, and our mission and ministry as Christians, should be seen in the light of this challenge.

In the parable of the talents, Jesus tells us how things work in God's kingdom:

> Then the man who had received one bag of gold came. 'Master,' he said, '... I was afraid and went out and hid your gold in the ground ...'
>
> His master replied, 'You wicked, lazy servant! ... You should have put my money on deposit with the bankers, so that when I

returned I would have received it back with interest.

'So take the bag of gold from him and give it to the one who has ten bags. For whoever has will be given more, and they will have an abundance. Whoever does not have, even what they have will be taken from them. And throw that worthless servant outside.'
Matthew 25:24-30

Why did the Lord disapprove of this man's actions? It was because he hid what God had given him to use.

In order to deepen our relationship with God, we need to pray, worship, study the Bible and seek His presence in our lives.

This leaflet describes some of the components needed for us to become kingdom people.

Components for growth

1. A life of intimate relationship with God through, prayer, worship and study of the Bible.
2. Learning with and from others.
3. Being witnesses for Christ.
4 Ministering to others.
5. Serving in our community.

1. A life of intimate relationship with God through prayer, worship and study of the Bible

In Matthew 22:37-38, Jesus said, 'Love the Lord your God with all your heart and with all your soul and with all your mind. This is the first and greatest commandment.'

We are made for relationship with God, Jesus and the Holy Spirit. Deepening that relationship in closer intimacy must be our first priority, to hear and listen to God and be connected to an open heaven through prayer, the study of God's Word and revelation. We seek to know God's purposes for our lives in God's power, not on our own, and to be instruments of His kingdom. We must always remain connected to Jesus, the true vine (John 15:1), for without Him we can do nothing. Worshipping God needs to be done not only on an individual basis but also on a corporate basis. To know God, we need to spend time with Him daily and enjoy being in His presence and speaking to our Daddy, Father God. We can worship and sing songs to God alone and with others. Reading God's Word and allowing Him to reveal His truths to us is both a personal and a corporate activity in our churches. Here prayer, testimony and vibrant music and singing are expressed. All aspects of the service should reflect God's love, compassion, holiness of life, mercy and freedom in regard to the individual's intimacy with God, and service to the local community. Opportunities to attend retreats to rest from our busyness helps us to focus more on what God wants us to do and hear. We should be a people not acting out of a religious spirit but out of a conscious spiritual and personal walk with God.

Think about your relationship with God, and reflect on your intimacy with Him.

2. Learning with and from others

The church we attend should be a place where we seek God's heart and grace and encourage one another in our walk with God. It should be a place where, if possible, the power and the gifts of the Holy Spirit are demonstrated. The authenticity of the Word of God is preached, and a personal, intimate and conscious relationship with God is encouraged. There is also an expectation to realise our identity – who we are in Christ as His sons and daughters. Discipleship is a lifetime experience as we become more Christlike. It happens through both grace as we learn from others, and through discipline. Discipleship entails not only commitment to a life of prayer and to the study of the Bible, but also to discovering who we are in Christ and partaking in the supernatural life we have as heirs, sons and daughters of God.

Think about how you can increase your intimacy with God and how you can disciple and encourage others in church

3. Being witnesses for Christ

In Matthew 28:19, Jesus commanded His followers to go and make disciples wherever we go, and this includes our homes, streets, workplaces and the community. In Acts 1:8 Jesus called us to be His witnesses in the world. When we have a vibrant relationship with God, we cannot help but tell others of our joy and experiences with God. Witnesses give an account of what they have seen and experience. We are called to do the same. We do not need to be Bible scholars to describe to others what God has done for us in our lives. There is nothing more powerful than a personal testimony, as this demonstrates God's existence and His love and compassion towards us. We should be prepared to tell in a few minutes those who do not know God how we had an encounter with the living God. Being a witness for Christ is a fruit of Christian life.

Think about how you can be a witness and how you can share with others in a succinct way what God is doing in your life.

4. Ministering to others

In Matthew 22:39, Jesus talks about the second greatest commandment: 'Love your neighbour as yourself.' God expects us to love and care for others, and by so doing we demonstrate the kingdom of God on earth. Each of us within the body of Christ has God-given talents and gifts and a calling to witness and minister in Christ's name. We must discern how God wants us to use our spiritual and natural gifts in His service and seek His power to do so. We are to know the personal destiny and purpose for our lives and to work with others who have a similar calling. We are to use our talents and spiritual gifts to minister to the poor and to those who do not know Him. Kingdom people respond to this calling with grateful hearts and also with the generous offering of our time, our abilities and our financial resources to God and His church. There is no more fulfilling way to spend our lives.

Think about the gifts and talents you have been given and the ways in which you could use them to reach out to others.

5. Serving in our community

Jesus calls us to love both God and our neighbours. We are called to witness and demonstrate His love and compassion wherever we go. We live in a variety of communities. These include our families, our workplaces, our streets and our towns. Do our communities know by our witness and lifestyle that we are Christians? Do they see our love and care for them? Also, as Jesus indicated in Matthew 25:35 and Luke 4:18, we are commissioned to reach out to those who are physically poor and poor in spirit. We need to discern what the needs of our communities are and endeavour to meet these needs or to join others in doing all we can to show God's love, compassion and mercy. As members of the body of Christ, we are to work together with other churches to meet the tremendous needs of our community, to serve and offer acts of kindness and love.

Think about how you can actively serve in your community.

Kingdom people

Next steps

I will work harder to have a closer relationship with God by ....
....

I will pray ....
....

I will read the Bible ....
....

I will go to church ....
....

I will share my faith story with ....
....

I will give money to God by ....
....

I will serve my community by ....
....

Signed ....
Date ....

Appendix 5 (For the review of church leaders)
Being a kingdom church

A kingdom people within churches who are seeking to encounter God together

God's heart is to reconcile the world to Himself in Jesus. We are called to be 'kingdom people' and our churches are called to be 'kingdom churches'. Our churches should be places where His presence and His love and compassion are demonstrated, and places that lead people to seek God with all of their heart and where the whole Word of God is preached.

This leaflet describes the components for a kingdom church and suggests some of the ways in which church leaders can develop their churches in the way that God intends them to be. It also provides a tool to leaders to use to consider their current position and future actions.

Characteristics of a kingdom church

1. People can have an intimate relationship with God through prayer, worship and study of the Bible.
2. Its members learn and share with others.
3. They are effective witnesses for Christ.
4. They minister to others.

5. They serve in the community.

6. They are led by a team with a defined vision, objectives and expectations, which support a kingdom ministry with financial integrity.

7. They are dedicated to helping and equipping children and young people to belong and become effective Christians.

8. They are committed to making their buildings fit for purpose as spiritual and community resources.

1. People can have an intimate relationship with God through prayer, worship and study of the Bible

In Matthew 22:37-38, Jesus says, 'Love the Lord your God with all your heart and with all your soul and with all your mind. This is the first and greatest commandment.'

Our church services and ministries enable members to deepen their personal and intimate relationship with God, encouraging them to love God and to desire His presence in a greater way. They encourage or enable the members to hear His voice and to walk in faith, trust and dependency on His leading. They encourage the people to seek time daily to be with God and to be hungry and thirsty for Him. The church should encourage its members to study the Bible at home alone.

Church services should be occasions where people hear God's authentic Word preached and know how it can be practically implemented in their lives. There may be opportunities in the service for people to receive prophetic words. Music should enhance our worship of God in such a way that all members feel they can move closer to God and can relate to its style. The service encompasses the concept of the Trinity, including naming the Holy Spirit. The service encourages its members to know their identity in God and to live in its empowerment.

Kingdom churches combine worship and the people's intimacy with God with serving their communities. The style of worship may be modern and vibrant with multimedia presentation, perhaps a lot of instruments. On the other hand, churches with a quieter and more traditional form of worship may also be kingdom churches.

A church should ideally reflect the community it serves; for example, a church in an area where there are many elderly people may offer a more reflective and quieter style of service. A community with a lot of young people and children may respond more readily to a more modern style of service. Accessibility to the newcomer is of paramount importance, as is making newcomers feel welcome and comfortable

Criterion: That people are able to deepen their personal relationship with God through prayer, worship and study of the Bible. This should mean the whole of the Bible, which is respected as the authentic and inspired Word of God, a guide for our daily Christian lives.

❖ Prayer guides and Bible study notes are readily available for members to take to encourage personal devotional times.

❖ The church's programme includes opportunities for prayer and Bible study during the week (small groups, Bible study meetings, and so on).

- ❖ The church promotes and encourages people to pray with other Christians across the town for their local community, country and the world.

- ❖ The church regularly teaches God's Word and expounds the Scriptures in a practical and kingdom way.

- ❖ The importance of the gifts of the Holy Spirit is expressed for day-to-day use in the church and the community.

- ❖ The development of personal intimacy with God is taught.

- ❖ Acts of faith are seen and encouraged.

- ❖ Prayer precedes and accompanies all of the church's work.

- ❖ People are encouraged to develop and grow in their personal discipline of prayer and devotion.

- ❖ There is a recognition of the importance of prayer and a greater desire by the people to come together to pray, corporately and within small groups.

- ❖ The church regularly prays for its local community, town and other churches.

- ❖ The church regularly prays for the UK, the Queen, local and national government, and worldwide issues.

- ❖ There are opportunities in the services for the Holy Spirit to speak.

- There are opportunities in the services for the gifts of the Holy Spirit to be used, if this is a church where this concept is a familiar one.

- There is an expectation that people will meet with God in worship and be transformed by the experience.

- Bible-based teaching is expressed and people demonstrate its fruit in practical ways.

- Testimonies are encouraged in services.

- Music and singing incorporates thanksgiving, praise and worship and there is a mix of traditional and modern music with varying pace.

- Prayers focus on church members, local, national and world issues and needs.

- There are opportunities to pray and to support each other's needs.

- New people feel welcomed and comfortable in the church.

- There are opportunities to pray and minister for people.

- People are friendly and caring towards one another.

- There are regular times to celebrate Communion each month.

- There are opportunities of quietness to hear God's voice.

- People are encouraged and discipled to have a personal, intimate and conscious relationship with God.

2. Its members learn and share with others

The church we attend should be a place where we seek God's heart and grace and encourage one another in our walk with God. It should be a place where, if possible, the power and the gifts of the Holy Spirit are demonstrated. The authenticity of the Word of God is preached, and a personal, intimate and conscious relationship with God is encouraged. There is also an expectation to realise our identity of who we are in Christ as His sons and daughters. Discipleship is a lifetime experience as we become more Christlike. It happens both through grace as we learn from others and through discipline. Discipleship entails not only commitment to a life of prayer and to the study of the Bible, but also to discovering who we are in Christ and partaking in the supernatural life we have as heirs, sons and daughters of God.

Criterion: To be devoted to discipling one another.

❖ Discipleship training embraces the basics of the Christian faith, who we are in Christ, as well as the spiritual gifts of the Holy Spirit.

❖ There are opportunities for new Christians to attend discipleship training (such as the basics of being a Christian and baptismal classes) and one-to-one sessions.

❖ Members are encouraged to attend discipleship training.

❖ The church's programme includes the provision for small groups, mentoring and Bible study.

- ❖ Relationships are nurtured so that people feel accepted and are helped to grow in faith and to be effective in practical Christian living.

- ❖ There is a men's group in the church.

- ❖ There is women's group in the church.

- ❖ Short courses such as marriage preparation, marriage and parenting are available.

- ❖ There are opportunities for people to be accountable to each other.

- ❖ People are equipped to teach, preach and lead the singing, music and worship service.

3. They are effective witnesses for Christ

In Matthew 28:19, Jesus commanded His followers to go and make disciples wherever we go, and this includes our homes, streets, workplaces and the community. In Acts 1:8 we are called to be His witnesses in the world. When we have a vibrant relationship with God, we cannot help but tell others of our joy and experiences with God. Witnesses give an account of what they have seen and experience. We are called to do the same. We do not need to be Bible scholars to describe to others what God has done for us in our lives. There is nothing more powerful than a personal testimony, as this demonstrates God's existence and His love and compassion towards us. We should be prepared to tell in a few minutes those who do not know God how we had an encounter with the living God. Being a witness for Christ is a fruit of Christian life.

Criterion: To be equipped to witness and to lead people to Christ

❖ People are encouraged, equipped and trained to witness and to share Christ by telling their personal stories.

❖ People are encouraged and given opportunities to tell their stories of what God has done and is doing in their lives.

❖ Time is set aside for specific events that share the gospel with those on the fringes of or outside the church.

❖ An enquirers' group or course (such as Alpha) is regularly offered for those wanting to know more about the Christian faith.

❖ People are encouraged and equipped to witness to their neighbours, friends, family and work colleagues.

❖ People are encouraged to pray and meet the needs of others through acts of random kindness to show God's love and compassion for them.

❖ People are encouraged and given opportunities to use creative ministries (such as face-painting and drama) to share the gospel.

❖ The church regularly shares the needs of the local community and seeks to support and minister to these needs.

4. They minister to others

In Matthew 22:39, Jesus talks about the second greatest commandment: 'Love your neighbour as yourself.' God expects us to love and care for others and by so doing we demonstrate the kingdom of God on earth.

Our church services and ministries enable our members to deepen their love for other people, both friends and newcomers inside and outside the church.

Criterion: To be resourced and released to minister to others.

❖ The church and its people are open to the Spirit's leading about what they should be and do.

❖ The different gifts and experiences of everyone are valued, known and given expression in and beyond the life of the church they attend.

❖ The church supports ministries to the poor in their local town.

❖ People are encouraged and equipped to discover their personal calling and ministry to the poor and to seek and work with others to develop their destiny and purpose.

❖ Finances are given fairly to local and international ministries, so that these ministries are self-sustaining or funded through church partnerships, not donor or secular dependent.

❖ The church encourages and releases people to support local ministries (such as a food bank or a night shelter).

5. They serve in the community

Jesus calls us to love both God and our neighbours. The church encourages its members to reach out to people around them and to be God's witnesses; to demonstrate His love and compassion wherever they go and to be salt and light in their connected communities.

We should encourage church members to use their gifts, time and money to support, love and care for others, and to support those who are poor and vulnerable. In this way, they take both the first and second commandments of Jesus seriously by endeavouring to love God and their neighbours. As Jesus indicated in Matthew 25:34-36 and Luke 4:18 the church's commission is to reach out to those who are physically poor and poor in spirit. We need to discern what the needs of our community are and to meet these needs or to join others I doing all we can to show God's love, compassion and mercy. As the body of Christ and the united church we work together as one to meet the tremendous needs of our community, to serve and offer acts of kindness and love. It is a passion for the lost, for those who do not know Christ. We need to pray for them, meet their needs, build relationships and encourage them in their realisation of the gospel.

Criterion: To serve our community.

❖ The church has an outward-looking focus and engages with the whole life of the local community.

❖ The church works in partnership with others in order to meet the needs of local people.

- ❖ The church is used for ministries to the poor (such as debt support, working with the homeless).

- ❖ The church is used to supporting children's and youth ministries (such as Boys' and Girls' Brigades, Scouts).

- ❖ The church is passionate and prophetic about love, compassion, justice and freedom, locally and globally.

- ❖ The church offers hospitality, advice, prayer and support to the local community.

- ❖ The community knows about and actively engages with the church.

6. They are led by a team with a defined vision, objectives and expectations, which support a kingdom ministry with financial integrity

Jesus supported a team ministry approach by choosing, discipling and equipping a group of twelve disciples (later apostles) to support His ministry. Seven deacons, who were Spirit-filled men, were chosen to administer the affairs of the apostles (Acts 6:3). Moses chose leaders to care for the nation of Israel (Exodus 18:21-26). Growing and developing churches have leaders with apostolic, prophetic, evangelistic, teaching and pastoral giftings. Maintenance leaderships usually operate with pastoral and administrative functions. Kingdom leaderships desire to see evidence of the Holy Spirit moving in the church and for the people to be Spirit filled and to have an intimate relationship with God, rather than to be of a religious spirit.

Criterion: To be led by a team with a defined vision, objectives and expectations, which supports a kingdom ministry with financial integrity.

❖ The church's vision, objectives and expectations are clearly written down and implemented.

❖ There is a certainty that God has spoken and commissioned the ministries with which the church is involved, and it is not just a good idea or a response to need.

❖ The leadership demonstrate apostolic, prophetic, evangelistic, teaching and pastoral giftings. The prophetic is valued and guides decision-making at key times.

❖ There is ongoing prayer and openness to the Holy Spirit's leading.

❖ The team of workers are chosen because of a personal sense of call and appropriate giftings, not because of personal ambition.

❖ Leaders meet weekly or fortnightly to pray, seek God and lead the church.

❖ There is a clear leadership structure with good accountability and transparency.

❖ The team freely gives of its time to the life of the church and its ministries (not just on Sundays and other specific times in the week).

❖ The team provides pastoral support.

- ❖ The team provides effective teaching and leads appropriate services of worship.

- ❖ The leadership know the talents and spiritual giftings of the church's members and deploys them effectively for the sake of building God's kingdom in the church and local area.

- ❖ The church has clear procedures for record keeping with regard to the handling of money.

- ❖ Budgets are prepared and overseen, and information is shared openly with the church.

- ❖ People give to churches and ministries in an honourable and spiritual way.

- ❖ The church gives fairly to ministries inside and outside the church and abroad.

- ❖ The church regularly gives money to churches working together to support the local community.

7. They are dedicated to helping and equipping children and young people to belong and become effective Christians

Children and young people are not only the church of tomorrow; they are also the church of today. Jesus showed preferential consideration for children, and we must do the same. If we do not do so, not only will the future of our churches be in doubt, but they will also be impoverished in the present. God uses children and young adults in the same ways as He uses adults, and they need to be equipped for works of service here and now. We have much to learn from children and young people and much to offer them. They too can pray for the sick, and they can disciple other children and young adults.

Criterion: To be dedicated to helping and equipping children and young people to belong and become effective Christians.

❖ Children and young people are involved in small group ministry.

❖ Provision is made for children and young people to learn about the Christian life during Sunday services.

❖ Children and young people are involved in the life of the church (for example, in the music group).

❖ Provision is exciting and uses modern, multimedia resources where possible.

❖ Children and young people are equipped alongside adults to provide ministry to others (for example, in using their gifts of the Holy Spirit).

❖ Services reflect the inclusion of children and young people.

❖ There is a strategy for equipping children and young people in the church.

❖ There is a strategy for engaging with unchurched children and young people.

❖ Opportunities for children and young people to join with other churches are supported.

- ❖ The church supports opportunities for leaders and workers to work and share with other leaders in the town.

- ❖ The church engages with other churches to minister to children and young people (for example, children's or youth clubs).

- ❖ The church actively reaches out to unchurched children and youth (for example, through youth cafés, work in schools).

8. They are committed to making their buildings fit for purpose as spiritual and community resources

Our churches are sometimes seen as a burden, with rising maintenance and operating costs and concerns for health and safety regulations and security. However, they are blessings and God-given resources to the Christians attending them and for the community. Too many churches are locked for all but a few hours a week when they could be a vital spiritual and community resource. We should seek to do what we can to enable them to be used to their full potential for the praise of God and for local residents, caring and ministering to the poor and for the common good.

Criterion: To be committed to making buildings fit for purpose as spiritual and community resources.

- ❖ The church building is accessible during daylight hours.

- ❖ Prayers are offered in the church building on a daily basis.

- ❖ The building has been sensitively adapted so that the church is able to offer hospitality to all kinds of groups, meetings and activities.

- ❖ There is a strategy for encouraging and welcoming visitors to the church throughout the week and on Sundays.

- ❖ There is a structure of keeping in contact with visitors to the church.

- ❖ Where there is a caretaking issue, there is a willingness to work with other churches to support the opening of the church.

- ❖ Secular groups use the church, encouraging community engagement.

- ❖ Schools regularly visit the church for educational purposes.

- ❖ Activities in the church throughout the week actively seek to engage the community.

- ❖ The building is used to serve the poor in the community (for example, for a food bank, for the homeless, debt support).

Kingdom church tool

My church is:

For each of the nine characteristics, please rate your church as follows:

6 this is a strength
5 there is much evidence of this
4 we are making progress in this area
3 there is some evidence of this
2 there are only a few signs of this
1 this is a weakness

Characteristic	Rating					
	6	5	4	3	2	1
1. People can have an intimate relationship with God through prayer, worship and study of the Bible.						
2. Its members learn and share with others.						
3. They are effective witnesses for Christ.						
4. They minister to others.						

5. They serve in the community.						
6. They are led by a team with a defined vision, objectives and expectations, which support a kingdom ministry with financial integrity.						
7. They are dedicated to helping and equipping children and young people to belong and become effective Christians.						
8. They are committed to making their buildings fit for purpose as spiritual and community resources.						

Appendix 6
Prophetic words

This section contains a selection of prophecies received in the early years about how God would speak to and work through the churches in Barking. These are word-pictures and symbolic images from God, indicating the ways in which He is going to bring about His purposes. Some of them have been fulfilled in part; most have yet to come to fruition. They are God's Word to us and they inspire us to look to the future. Further prophetic words have been received regularly year by year, which are too many to be included.

Words of God over Barking, 2009–2010

1. New wineskins

> 'Neither do people pour new wine into old wineskins. If they do, the skins will burst; the wine will run out, and the wineskins will be ruined. No, they pour new wine into new wineskins, and both are preserved.'
> *Matthew 9:17*

2. A seed needs to die before it can grow and produce fruit

> 'Very truly I tell you, unless a grain of wheat falls to the ground and dies, it remains only a single seed. But if it dies, it produces many seeds.'
> *John 12:24*

Both these prophecies referred to the old structure of churches meeting together before BCU was formed. The existing organisation of united churches had 'died', in that it had collapsed; the new BCU and its ministries was to be the 'many seeds'.

3. Rebuild the city and walls of Barking

Churches need to work together (next to each other) and protect each other if we are to do this.

> 'If it pleases the king and if your servant has found favour in his sight, let him send me to the city in Judah … so that I can rebuild it.'
> *Nehemiah 2:5*

All the clans/tribes worked side by side to build the walls.

> From that day on, half of my men did the work, while the other half were equipped with spears, shields, bows and armour. The officers posted themselves behind all the people of Judah who were building the wall. Those who carried materials did their work with one hand

and held a weapon in the other, and each of the builders wore his sword at his side as he worked.

Nehemiah 4:16-18

4. RCCG prophecy (Redeemed Christian Church of God, a Nigerian organisation)

A white person would come with a vision to unify the church and this would lead to transformation and growth of the white Christian population.

5. Words given to Mick

'Establish my kingdom in the city. Build it on kingdom principles, not by man-made structures.'

We are entering the Day of Jubilee (in Leviticus 25, the Year of Jubilee is a time of blessing).

6. Light in darkness

We received a picture of small lights being turned on in Barking. These small lights would become one big light. This big light would replace the darkness over Barking.

7. Trickle of water

We received a picture of a trickle of water coming out of a rock, becoming a stream, then a river, then a waterfall and finally an ocean. The interpretation of this picture was that things will start small and grow into something bigger, as resources are pooled.

8. Together

The word for the nation is the need to work TOGETHER. This is also a word for the church.

Words of God over Barking, 2011

1. Barking – Son of the King.
2. God's favour is upon Barking when we are united.
3. 'I have opened doors and opportunities out of My favour.'
4. 'If my church is moved into the community, I will bring healing and blessing.'
5. 'I will cause my people to be pregnant with dreams and projects to touch my city.'
6. 'The time has come for the church of the city to raise a fanfare of trumpets to the Lord and I will bring down the walls of the city you are surrounding. It will be like ancient times and Jericho.'

Words of God over Barking, 2012

1. You are a royal priesthood over Barking.
2. 'You are my watchman over the city.'
3. 'I want to turn the desert of Barking into a green, fertile land.'
4. The church needs to work harder together to be a family.
5. The church is a hosepipe with holes. As the churches come together the holes will be repaired and water (the Holy Spirit) will gush out over Barking.
6. A spiritual void been left after the Olympics. God wants to fill it with His kingdom and weighted presence.
7. Picture of a person receiving a gold medal and someone trying to steal it. Don't let Satan take back what we have already gained. Claim it and retain it.
8. Love is the key to taking Barking. Words and deeds show God's love.

9. Barking's jewel is the church. The jewel's prism reflects light from heaven; different lights colour different directions. Our job is to receive and distribute the light. We all need to be in the correct position to reflect the light.

10. A picture of a dark cloud over the River Thames. Praise brings the sun. Mighty things are to happen in 2013.

11. God wants the church to bottle laughter (like the laughter of a child). Shake off the clouds and rejoice.

12. A picture of a star over Barking. People will be drawn to Barking and God's presence.